GLIMPSES OF BASTI; THE HEALING ART

DR VRUSHALI S SWAMI, DR ASWATHI C K & DR SANTOSH I SWAMI

Contents

Preface

Ayurveda, the ancient science of life and holistic healing, has offered a profound understanding of health and disease for millennia. Among its diverse treatment modalities, "Basti"—a form of therapeutic enema—stands out as one of the most powerful and revered therapies in the Panchakarma system. As a treatment that both purifies and nourishes the body, "Basti" holds a unique place in the management of various disorders and the preservation of well-being.

In "Glimpses of Basti", we aim to offer readers an in-depth exploration of this therapeutic approach. Our intent is to provide a comprehensive resource that will serve as both an academic guide and a practical manual for students, practitioners, and anyone interested in the healing power of Ayurveda.

This work is divided into various sections that cover the classical references, the types and formulations used, and its wide-ranging applications in both preventive and curative aspects of health.

Our collaborative effort stems from the belief that "Basti" therapy, though ancient, remains highly relevant today. It addresses not only physical ailments but also imbalances in the mind and spirit, aligning with the Ayurvedic philosophy of treating the individual as a whole. Through this book, we hope to illuminate the wisdom of our ancestors and present it in a way that is accessible and applicable to the modern reader.

We are deeply grateful to the scholars, practitioners, and institutions that have contributed to the knowledge of Basti therapy, and it is our privilege to share this knowledge with you. It is our hope that "Glimpses of Basti" will serve as a valuable addition to the growing body of Ayurvedic literature and inspire further study and practice in this remarkable therapy.

With warm regards,

Dr Vrushali S Swami, Dr Aswathi C K & Dr Santosh I Swami

PREFACE

Acknowledgements

We would like to express our deepest gratitude to all those who have supported us in the creation of this book, "Glimpses of Basti". This work is a culmination of years of dedication to the study and practice of Ayurveda, and it would not have been possible without the guidance, encouragement, and contributions of many individuals.

First and foremost, we extend our heartfelt thanks to our teachers and mentors in the field of Ayurveda. Your wisdom, teachings, and unwavering support have been our foundation, inspiring us to delve deeper into the profound knowledge of this ancient science.

We are also immensely grateful to our colleagues and peers for their insightful feedback and for enriching our understanding through collaborative discussions. Your camaraderie has been invaluable throughout this journey.

A special thanks to our families for their patience, encouragement, and constant belief in our vision. Your love and support gave us the strength to see this project through to completion.

Lastly, we would like to thank our readers. It is for you that we have undertaken this endeavour to explore the therapeutic aspects of Basti in Ayurveda. We hope this book serves as a meaningful resource for both students and practitioners alike, and that it deepens your understanding of this important treatment modality.

Thank you

ACKNOWLEDGEMENTS

CHAPTER I

Basti – general introduction

The term "basti" refers to the therapeutic enema technique. It is one of the five panchakarma purifying techniques. Literally, the word "basti," also written "basti," means "bladder". The urinary bladder is referred to as the basti from an anatomical perspective. The ancient practice of administering enema therapy through an animal's bladder—usually a goat or a buffalo—gives the therapy its name, basti. It is the finest treatment for vata dosha diseases. Basti is regarded as the most effective form of panchakarma since vata dosha has a major role in the development of ailments.

It refers to a medicated enema with decoction, oils, or any other fluid either in the rectum or as part of therapeutic care. Enema administered through an anterior orifice, such as the urethra or vagina, is referred to as "uttara basti." Unction therapy makes use of local therapeutic techniques including applying heated oils or medicinal substances to the affected body area. As a prefix to the word "basti," these procedures are referred to by the name of the affected part. For instance, "janu basti" refers to applying a warm medication to the knee joint, while "kati basti" refers to applying it to the lower back. 'Basti' most frequently refers to a per rectal enema.

The application of the Basti (enema) is considered by sages of authority to be the best of all remedies since it serves to control, soothe, and cleanse various Dosha (body humors) due to its variety of functions and comparison to many types of medical medications.It is regarded as the primary treatment for Vata disorders. It is effective in treating illnesses brought on by disturbed Pitta, Kapha, Rakta, any two, or all three of them. Niruha Basti is one of the varieties of Basti that are frequently employed by practitioners because it removes Dosha from the system, treats sickness, regenerates the body, and promotes lifespan. Basti formulation is one of several key determinants that affect Niruha Basti's ability to produce the intended result.

The materials, their dosage, attributes, order and technique of mixing, qualities of well-prepared Basti, and justification for sequential mixing have all been underlined in the primary classical books of Ayurveda. It is pointless, like the efforts of an ass carrying a load of sandalwood, for a man to study the entire Shastra (classical book) and yet be unable to explain it in a way that is understandable to others. Therefore, it's crucial to examine the complete Niruha Basti formulation from classical writings and comprehend its justification for practical implementation.

BASTI

According to Ayurvedic traditional literature, basti, the best treatment in shodhana, is regarded as one of the most crucial remedies for numerous ailments. It is the most effective method of treatment for all vata-related illnesses. Asthapana basti, also known as niruha basti, is a form of basti in which the main ingredient is a decoction, whereas anuvasana basti's main ingredient is oil or another sneha (oleaginous material).

Etymology and derivation

The word 'basti' is derived from the root 'vas' with suffix 'tich'. 'Vas' is having the following meanings

- To reside or to stay or to dwell/to cover/to move or motion
- Vas nivase: to reside, to stay, to dwell
- Vas achadane: means to cover, to coat
- Vas snehachadane praharaneshu: covering of Sneha for the elimination.
- Vas vasane surabhikarane: to produce the effect of pleasant smell.
- Vaste avrinoti mutram : organ which covers the urine.
- Nabhisya adhobhage mutradhare sthane: organ situated below the umbilicus which retains the urine.
- Vast gandhe ardane : vast gandhe- mala, ardane- Yacane cha: to beg/to draw mala out of the body.
- Oushadha danarthe dravyabhedhe: an instrument for administration of medicine.

Definition

1.Definition as a panchakarma

- "nabhi pradesham katiparswa kukshim gatwa sakrt dosha chayam vilodya Samsnehya kaya sapureesha dosa samyak sukheneti cha ya:sa basti"
- "Bastina deeyate bastim va puravamnvetyato basti"

The procedure in which either basti is used for the administration of drugs or drugs that are administered reaches the basti initially

- "bastibhirdhiyate yasmat tasmat bastiriti smriti:"

2. Basti as an organ

- According to Charaka it is one among the Dasa prana ayatana and Panchadasa kostanga
- According to Astanga hridaya it is one among the Dasa jeevita dhamani
- In Cha.Chi: Trimarmeeya chikitsa: Basti is one among the Trimarma.The prana is dependent and residing in the trimarma. Any disease occurring in these sites are considered as Mahagada.

3. As an instrument

- According to Su.Chi 35/3 "basti karma tu mutradharaputakena sadhya karmam"
- Bladder of animals are used to perform Basti. Hence , the term Basti was used.

General considerations of Basti
1.Prime treatment of Vata dosha
'' vatolbaneshu dosheshu vate va bastirishyate....(Ah.Su)
According to Sarvanga sundara:
'' tena vatasya bastirgudapranidheyasnehakwathadi paramousadham''
2. Age of the individual

- According to Kasyapa : "adhastano annabhokta cha chayadata.."

A discussion in Rajaputriya sidhi adhyaya in Kasyapa Samhita regarding the appropriate age for administration of Basti.

- In context of Bala chikitsa, Ah.Utt-

''basti sadhye virekena'': when conditions requiring virechana occurs. In children, Basti is the choice Virechana should be administered to the dhatri only

- In Ah.Su,-'' aajanma maranam sastam pratimarshastu bastivat''

The length of Basti netra in Astanga Hridaya for different age groups, the term une abde pancha....
Niruha matra for a child of 1 year is mentioned – 1 prakuncha
3. Based on the site of disease/ roga adhistana

- Basti can be administered both in sareerika and manasika vikara

Eg -Basti is indicated – sakhagata koshtagata....

- Basti is indicated for Unmada and Apasmara.

4. Based on Ritu

- Asthapana is indicated in varsha ritu according to Ashtanga hridaya
- Vamanadi is indicated in Vasanta ritu according to Cha.Su
- Indicates the use of basti both for Swastha as well as Atura

5. Route of administration
Basti bypasses the liver and acts by menas of the enteric nervous system and the rich supply by the plexus in the rectum and anal canal.Hence, basti can be considered as

a mode of treatment that can be chosen when there is a need to spare the stomach and liver.Basti is also a mode of treatment for diseases of urinary bladder and urethra.

6. Management of Asthi dhathu kshaya

Ksheera or sarpi processed with tikta rasa dravya used for various purposes especially basti.

Importance of Basti

- Basti is considered as "ardha chikitsa '' by Charaka Samhita.
- Acts on diseases occurring through all roga marga – bahya,abhyantara and madhyama.
- As vata is responsible for the vikshepa and sanghata of vit,mootra and pittadi, basti is most suitable for the restoration of equilibrium .
- Caters to diseases affecting various systems like – nervous sytem,orthopeadics, colic, reproductive system etc.
- Best choice for repleneshiment of lost vitality.
- Produces significant impact in physical, mental and psychosomatic illness

Application of Basti in Astanga

KAYACHIKITSA

''Bastirvaya sthapayita sukhayurbalagnimedha swaravarna krit cha

Sarvarthakari sisu vridha yoonam niratyaya: sarvagadahapascha

Vitshleshma pittaanilamutra karshee

Dardyavaha: sukrabalapradascha

Viswaksthitham dosachayam nirasya

Sarvan vikaran samayennirooha"(Cha.Si.1/27-28)

- According to Chakrapani: vaya:sthapanatwam cha srota: sudhikaratwat
- According to Kasyapa samhitha:

'' bastidanat nasti chikitsa angasukhavaha"
''tadha kaphasya pittasya malanam cha rasasya cha
Vikshepane samharane vayorevatra Karanam
Jeta chasya pravridhasya bastitulyo n kashchana
Tadupaardham chikitsaya: sarvam vatachiktisitam"
(Ka. Khi. 8/5) Bastivisheshaneeya
Vata is responsible for the expulsion or unification of kapha, pitta,excreta etc . Basti is the best treatment for vata.

- According to Su. Chi. 4/20

'' Sarvangagatam ekangasthitham va api sameeranaam
runadhi kevalo bastivayur vegamivachala"
Just as big mountains create a barrier to the fast moving speed of
wind, the vata dosa – localized or generalised can be overcome by
Basti.

- According to Cha.Si.10/5

''karmanyad bastim samam na vidyate seegram sukhavishodhitwat
Aaswapatarpana tarpana yogaccording ha niratyatwacha

- According to Su.Chi.35

'' iha khalu bastirnanavidha dravyasamyogat dosanam samsodhanam samsanam sangrahani karoti"

Basti is capable of producing multiple effects like sodhana, samsana and sangrahi.

2. Basti in Bala chikitsa

According to Kasyapa:

'' sisunamasisunam cha basti karmamrutham yatha bhisajamartha yasassi sisorayu: praja pitu:

Basti improves the longevity and strength of children and bestows child to infertile individuals

3. Basti in gyneacological and obstetric conditions

Susrutha – asthapana basti – 8th month of pregnancy

Vagbhata – anuvasana basti – 8th month

Charaka – anuvasana basti – 9th month

Treatment -yoni vayapth ,Vataja sukra dushti,nashtartava (Su)

According to Kasyapa,

''yasam cha garbha: sramsante jata va na drida suta:''

Basti- preventing abortions

4. Basti in Salyatantra

Best option for management of Marma,Bhagna chikitsa

One among sashti upakrama of vrana

5. Role of basti in rasayana and vajikarana

According to Su.Chi.35/3-4

''ksheena sukram vajikaroti, krisham brimahayati, sthula karsayati,

chakshu preenayati, valipalitamapahanti, vaya: sthapayati.Sareeropachaya varnam balamarogyamayusha: kurute"

CHAPTER II

Classification of basti

Basti can be classified based on different characteristics
On the basis of procedure

1. Enema with decoctions (Niruha basti)
2. Enema with unctuous substances (Anuvasana basti)
3. Enema through urethral or vaginal route (Uttarabasti)[Cha.si 10/8]

On the basis of site of administration
The basti can be broadly classified into internal and external based on the site of administration

1. Administered into colon through anal route (pakvashayagata basti)
2. Administered into uterus through vagina (garbhashayagata basti)
3. Administered into urinary bladder through urethra (mutrashayagata basti)
4. Administered over wounds for cleaning purpose (vrana basti) [Su.Sa.Chikitsa Sthana 35/11]

On the basis of pharmaco-therapeutic action
The enema therapy is classified based on the basis of karma

1. Dosha aggravating enema (utkleshana basti)
2. Dosha purificatory enema (shodhana basti)

3. Dosha pacifying enema (shamana basti)[Sha.Uttarardha.6/17-19]

On the basis of number of basti

The enema therapy is classified based on specific schedule

1. Karma basti: Total 30 basti sessions with 12 decoction (niruha) and 18 unctuous (anuvasana basti)
2. Kala basti: Total 16 basti sessions with 06 decoction (niruha) and 10 unctuous (anuvasana basti)
3. Yoga basti: Total 8 basti sessions with 3 decoction (niruha) and 5 unctuous (anuvasana basti)[Cha.Si 1/47-49]

On the basis of total quantity

Some enemas are classified based on the total quantity of ingredients. The proportion of ingredients and total amount of enema are calculated using the measurement "prasruta," where one prasruta is equal to 96 ml. Decoction enema can be taken up to a maximum of 1152 milliliters (12 prasruta). According to The Indian Ayurvedic Formulary(IAF) the dosage for one prasruta is 96 milliliters. Ayurveda states that each person's posology is unique.

Here 'prasruta' is defined as the dosage of liquid in the patient's hollowed palm. [Gayadasa on Su.Sa.Chikitsa Sthana 35/7]In a study conducted on 100 participants, one prasruta of Madhutailika basti (a type of decoction enema) is standardized as 26.4ml.

A few examples are as follows:

- Twelve prasruta (1152 ml) termed as 'Dwadasaprasrutika basti'
- Nine prasruta (864ml)termed as 'Navaprasruta basti/ padahina basti'
- Five prasruta (480 ml) termed as 'Pachaprasrutika basti'

Based on the chief ingredient

Some enemas are known by their chief ingredient. A few examples are as follows:

- Enema with equal quantity of honey and oil is termed as 'Madhutailika basti'
- Ksheera basti is the basti in which ksheera is the main content.

CHAPTER III

Mode of action

Basti has a variety of effects, and depending on other variables, this route of medication administration may have both anabolic (Brihana) and catabolic (Karshana) effects.The majority of Ayurvedic medications are taken orally. However, there are times when taking the normal approach is not ideal or practical. Although they differ in many ways, the oral and rectal routes both originate from the gastrointestinal system. The main functional distinction between the oral and rectal routes, or the large and small intestine, is that the oral route requires the medicine to go through the digestive process, whereas the rectal route does not. Rectal medication administration is the primary method of drug delivery in modern scientific techniques. Opioids are typically used for severe pain brought on by cancer treatment.

Ayurvedic view

all organs related to Basti Karma are Sadhyo Pranahara Marmas, by virue of Agneya guna which it posess it may help to transport the Basti Veerya more easily. The provided Basti arrives in Nabhi Pradesha, where the Veerya may be carried to the entire body via the aforementioned Dhamanis, Siras, and Srothas. More over NiruhaBasti is a uniform mixture of Makshika, Lavana, Sneha, Kalka and Kwatha. The Makshika and Lavana will help in KaphaChedana and Vilayana.Saindhava by it's Sukshma, Theekshna, and Vyavayi guna will reach to minute channels of the body. The many Dravyas utilized in making basti have varying qualities; some may be soluble in water, while others may be soluble in fat, and as such, they may be absorbed in different ways. The Kalka used in Basti help to attain the particular consistency which may be responsible for retaining Basti for a while for its function. Snehana causes Dosha Vishyandana and Swedana cause Srothomukha Visodhana. Both of them help to easily eliminate the imbalanced Dosha. Sukhoshnata is important intran action of Basti. There are lots of similes in our classics which beautifully explain the mode of action of Basti. The Basti stays in Pak-vashaya drags the Doshas from whole body just like the sun which resides in the sky evaporates the water from the earth surface. as those rays are strong and penetrating. Similarly the Teekshna, Ushna, Vyavayi oushadha used in Basti help to drag the vitiated Doshas present throughout the body. When a cloth is immersed in water mixed with a dye, the cloth will take the colour of dye only from water; like that, the given Basti will take out the vitiated Doshas from body. This explain the specificity of Basti. Even though the Basti reaches upto Pakvashaya, the Veerya of Basti is transported to all of the body; just like the water poured to root of the plant reaches to whole plant. We can make certain inferences on the basis of all these factors. The Basti is given to Vata Sthana and so it can alleviate the Vata at its'own site. As the Vata is brought under control the disease itself is cured, because without the major causative factor, the disease itself does not have any existence.

Modern view-mode of action

The therapeutic effect of Basti is the best evi-dence for its mode of action. But in contem-porary science action of Basti remain as a great dilemma. We can postulate certain hy-pothesis on the basis of mode of action. They are;

- **Absorption mechanism**
- **Neural Stimulation**
- **Chemical Stimulation**
- **Mechanical Stimulation**

- **Absorption mechanism**

Absorption of drugs from rectal epithelium involves two routes from epithelium: the transcellular route and paracellular route. Lipophilicity is necessary for the transcellular route, therefore sneha dravya, which is employed in Basti, encourages this kind of absorption. In paracellular route, drug diffuses through space between epithelial cells thus it may be the route of absorption for decoction preparation. Drug properties like partition coefficient and molecular size affect the absorption of medications in the rectum. The usual causes of poor drug absorption are large molecular size, charge, small partition coefficient, and high hydrogen bond forming capabilities. The majority of colon contents are alkaline, and the colon absorbs alkaline liquids more readily than it does acid solutions. It is therefore hypothesized that the majority of basti kalpana, which have an alkaline character, are more easily absorbed.

Neural Stimulation

The "enteric nervous system" (ENS) is the network of nerve fibers that makes up the gastrointestinal tract. The ENS records experiences, sends and receives impulses, and reacts to a range of stimuli, just like the brain. The same neurotransmitters permeate and have an influence on its nerve cells. The sheaths of tissue lining the oesophagus to colon contain the gut brain (ENS). Thought of as a single unit, it is actually a network of neurons with the ability to act independently, learn, remember, and generate gut instincts. It also contains neurotransmitters and proteins that transmit messages between neurons, regulate bodily functions similar to those found in the brain, and form a complex circle. There are 100 million more neurons in the gut than there are in the spinal cord. Important neurotransmitters include nitric oxide, glutamate, norepinephrine, serotonin, and dopamine. By communicating with a tiny number of "command neurons," the brain communicates with the gut, sending up-and down-moving signals to the gut interneuron. The two layers of the intestine dubbed the "myenteric plexus" and the "submucosal plexus" contain both interneurons and command neurons. The CNS and ENS cooperate with one another. Basti stimulation (either through chemo or mechano receptors) may activate the relevant area of the CNS, which causes the consequence to occur as expected.

Again it is not mandatory for a drug to stay in long time contact to the receptor e.g. like in Pro-ton Pump inhibitor where drug interact and flush out from circulation, it is known as "HIT AND RUN MODULE" of pharmacodynamics. Same module of pharmacody-namics may be hypothesized for Niruha Basti. There is close resemblance in the func-tioning of Vata Dosha and nervous system and Basti is prescribed as the best remedy for Vata.It again validates the efficacy of Basti karma on nervous system

- **Chemical and mechanical stimulation:**

Niruha Basti is hyper osmotic solu-tion which causes movement of solvent from cells of colon to the lumen containing Basti Dravya facilitates the absorption of endotoxin and produce detoxification during elimination. Kalka used in the Basti has got irritant property along with other ingredi-ents which may induce colonic distention. The distention stimulates pressure which produces evacuatory reflex. The sigmoidal, rectal and anal regions of large intestine are considerably better supplied with parasym-pathetic fibers than other part of intestine; they are mainly stimulatory in action and function especially in defecation reflexes. A volume of about 100 cc of gas is estimated to be present in the tract which is readily ex-pelled by Basti. Even though the Basti given is expelled out immediately as such or mixed with feces, the Veerya of Basti is spread throughout the body by the Vata. From this we can understand that the action of Basti is possible through nervous stimulation so that within seconds itself the action of Basti is spread. Certain mechanical or chem-ical stimulation is responsible for the action of Basti. Both of them cause nervous stimulation and thus produces the effect.

Gut Microflora

The gut microflora, often known as the gut microbial population, naturally exists in the human gut. The primary metabolic function of colonic microflora throughout the digestive process involves the fermentation of indigestible food remnants and mucus released by the epithelium. Carbohydrate fermentation occurs and is one of the colon's main sources of energy. The colon's (the later portion of the gut) has less accessible substrate for digestion, a pH that gradually approaches neutral, an increased importance for putrefactive processes, and stable bacterial populations. They also play significant role in certain vitamin synthesis. Absorption of ions like calcium, magnesium, and iron in colon is improved by carbohydrate fermentation and production of short-chain fatty acids, especially acetate, propionate, and butyrate. Differentiation of epithelial cells is also hugely influenced by colon microorganisms. All three major short-chain fatty acids also stimulate epithelial cell proliferation and differentiation in the large and small bowel in vivo which may enhance the absorption and metabolic process. Thus, it can be inferred that, in last part of intestine although there is no enzyme but some of important metabolic processes conducted by the flora of colon which may play role in basti process also.

Gut brain axis

Although Enteric Nervous System (ENS) was discovered 150 years ago, but importance of ENS was recognized in the recent 20-30 years with modern techniques and discoveries. Connections of ENS with CNS are previously thought to be only regulated by autonomic nervous system. It is a well known fact that it has same tissues as central nervous system (CNS) during fetal development. ENS has many structural and chemical similarities to the brain. Even when vagal supply is severed it continues to function way because of its own nervous system and can operate autonomously, thus also called as Second brain.

In enteric nervous system 30 neurotransmitters are found, which are identical to neurotransmitter found in CNS, such as acetylcholine, dopamine, and serotonin. Almost 90% serotonin, 50% of the dopamine of body lies in gut. Gastrointestinal tract was previously known to only have the function of digestion controlled by Central nervous system.

Now when Gut- Brain Axis (GBA) theory is well established, mechanisms underlying GBA communications involve neuroimmuno-endocrine mediators. Gut microflora also contributes in gut Brain axis.

CHAPTER IV

Clinical aspects of basti

Basti is commonly used alone or along with Ayurveda medication, in all Vata Vyadhi (neurological disorders) & is also indicated in various diseases . it is an ultimate remedy for psycho-somatic disease.

Indications of basti

"सर्वाङ्गैकाङ्गककुक्षिरोगवातवर्चोमूत्रशकुरसङ्गबलवर्णमांसरेतःक्षय
दोषाध्मानानाङ्गसुप्तिकिरमिकोष्ठोदावर्तशुद्धातिसार-
पर्वभेदाभितापप्लीहगुल्मशूलहृद्रोगभगन्दरोन्माद
ज्वरबुध्नशिरःकर्णशूलहृदयपार्श्वपृष्ठकटीग्रहवेपनाक्षेपक
गौरवातलाघवरजःक्षयार्तववैषम्याग्निसि्फग्जिानजङ्घोरुगुल्फ-
पार्ष्णिपिरपदयोनिबिाहुवङ्गुलिसितनान्तदन्तनखपर्वास्थिशूल
शोषस्तम्भान्त्रकूजपरिकिर्तिकाल्पाल्पसशब्दोग्रगन्धोत्थानादयो
[१]
वातव्याधयो विशिषेण महारोगाध्यायोक्ताश्च; एतेष्वास्थापनं
प्रधानतममतियुक्तं वनस्पतिमूलच्छेदवत्||१६||"(Cha.si.2/16)

Sarvaanga roga	Paralysis of the whole body
Ekaanga roga	Paralysis of side of body
Kukshi roga	Disorder of abdomen
Vata sanga	Retention of flatus
Varcho sanga	Retention of feces
Mootra sanga	Retention of urine
Shukra sanga	Retention of semen
Bala kshaya	Diminution of strength
Varna kshaya	Diminution of complexion
Mamsa kshaya	Diminution of muscle tissue
Retah kshaya	Diminution of semen
Doshaadhmaana	Tympanitis
Anga supti	Numbness of body parts
Krimikoshtha	Parasitic infestation of intestine
Udaavarta	Disorder due to reverse movement of the vata
Shuddhaatisaara	Diarrhea without association of ama
Parvabheda	Tearing pain in joints
Abhitaapa	Feeling of burning sensation
Pleeha roga	Splenic disorder
Gulma roga	Abdominal lump

table 1.1 indications of basti

Shula roga	Colic pain
Hridroga	Heart disease
Bhagandara	Fistula in ano
Unmada roga	Psychotic disorders
Jwara	Fever
Bradhna roga	Inguinal swelling
Shirahshula	Headache
Karnashula	Earache
Hridaya graha	Stiffness in heart
Paarshva graha	Stiffness in sides
Prishtha graha	Stiffness in back
Kati graha	Stiffness in waist
Vepana aarta	Suffering from tremor
Aakshepaka aarta	Suffering from convulsions
Gauravaarta	Suffering from heaviness
Atilaaghavaarta	Suffering from excessive lightness
Rajah-kshayaarta	Suffering from amenorrhea
Vishamaagni	Irregular power of digestion
Sphik-shula-shosha-stambha	Pain, atrophy and stiffness of hip

table 1.2 indications of basti

Jaanu-shula-shosha-stambha	Pain, atrophy and stiffness of knee-joints
Janghaa-shula-shosha-stambha	Pain, atrophy and stiffness of the calf region
Uru-shula-shosha-stambha	Pain, atrophy and stiffness of the thighs
Gulpha-shula-shosha-stambha	Pain, atrophy and stiffness of the ankles
Paarshni-shula-shosha-stambha	Pain, atrophy and stiffness of the heels
Prapada-shula-shosha-stambha	Pain, atrophy and stiffness of the feet
Yoni-shula-shosha-stambha	Pain, atrophy and stiffness of female genitals
Baahu-shula-shosha-stambha	Pain, atrophy and stiffness of arms
Anguli-shula-shosha-stambha	Pain, atrophy and stiffness of fingers
Stanaanta-shula-shosha-stambha	Pain, atrophy and stiffness of the periphery of the breasts
Danta-shula-shosha-stambha	Pain, atrophy and stiffness of teeth
Nakha-shula-shosha-stambha	Pain, atrophy and stiffness of nails
Parva-shula-shosha-stambha	Pain, atrophy and stiffness of joints

table 1.3 indications of basti

Asthi-shula-shosha-stambha	Pain, atrophy and stiffness of bones
Aantra koojana	Intestinal gurgling
Parikartika	Cutting pain in anal region
Alpaalpa-utthaana	Voiding stool in small quantity frequently
Sashabda-utthaana	Voiding stool with sound
Ugragandha-utthaana aadayo vyaadhyayah	(Diseases that cause) voiding stool with foul smell
Vata-vyaadhayo visheshena maharogadhyayoktah	Vatika disorders specially discussed in Maharoga Adhyaya of Charaka Samhita Sutra Sthana

table 1.4 indications of basti

Ashtangahridaya

"तेन साधयेत्‌|

गुल्‌मानाहखुडुप्‌लीहशुद्‌धातीसारशूलनिः||२||

जीर्‌णज्‌वरप्‌रतशि्‌यायशकु्‌रानलिमलग्‌रहान्‌|

वर्‌ध्‌माश्‌मरीरजोनाशान्‌ दारुणांश्‌चानलिमयान्‌||३||"(AH Su 19/ 02)

Susruta samhita

"तथा ज्‌वरातीसारतमिरिप्‌रतशि्‌यायशरिरोगाध्‌मिन्‌थार्‌दतिाक्‌षपेक पक्‌षाघातैकाङ्‌गसर्‌वाङ्‌गरोगाध्‌मानोदरयोनशिुलशर्‌कराशूल वृदू्‌ध्‌यपुदंशानाहमूतू्‌रकचू्‌छ्‌रगलु्‌मवातशोणतिवातमूतू्‌र पुरीषोदावर्‌तशकु्‌रार्‌तवसुतन्‌यनाशहृद्‌ध्‌नुमन्‌याग्‌रहशर्‌कराश्‌मरी मूढगर्‌भप्‌रभतृषि्‌[१] चात्‌यर्‌थमपुयज्‌यत ||५||"(Su.Su chi 35/ 5)

Special conditions mentioned by susruta :

- Timira, adhimantha
- sarkara soola
- Upadamsha,
- Mutrakrichra
- Stanya nasa
- Hanu graha, manya graha
- Mudagarbha
- according to Su- unmada is contraindicated for asthapana and anuvasana

<u>indicated conditions</u>
1.gulma

- "Vastikarmam param vidyad gulmaghnam, tat hi marutam"

swasthane prathamam jitwa sadyo gulmam apohati
tasmad abheekshnasho gulma niruhai: sanuvasanai:
prayujyamanai: saamyanti
vatapittakaphatmaka:"(A.Hr)
Here vasti acts on the sthana of vata – pakwasaya (Sa.Su)

- Condition to do vasti –

"Deepte agnou vatike gulme vibhandhe anila varchaso
brimhanayannapanani snighdoshnani pradapayet
puna: puna: snehapanam niruha: sanuvasana:
prayojya vataje gulme kaphapittanurakshina:"
here vasti can be utilised for anulomana so as to prevent
vata prakopa due to pratiloma gati
2. Anaha
According to Chakradatta

For pureesha nirodhaja udavarta

- '' udavarta kriya anahe same langhana pachanam''
- ''asthapane marutaje snigdha swinnasya shasyate''
- '' kshara vaitaranou vasti yunjyath tatra chikitsaka''
- Kshara or vaitarana basti can be used

3. vatashonita

- '' nirharedava malam tasya saghritai ksheeravastibhi:

na hi vast samam kinchit vata rakta chikitsita,''
(Cha.Chi)

- Here the purpose of vasti is- removal of biological toxins
- The clinical features are –

''vastvamkshana parswa uru parvasthi jatarartishu
udavarte cha sasyante niruha sanuvasana:''

- both anuvasana and niruha are indicated to relieve pain
  in various parts of the body.

4. Pleeha

- In general treatment of udara, virechana is the choice.
  But when there is udara adhmana even after
  administering vamana,Niruha with amla lavana drugs is
  adviced

- '' suviriktasya yasya syad adhmanam punareva cha

Su snighderamla lavaner niruhai: samupacharet''

(Ah.Chi15/41)

- when there is association of other dosa with vata in udara, teekshna vasti with gomutra should be administered.

5. sudha atisara

- A special vasti in atisara- Picha vasti

- ''ashantavityatisare picha basti: param hitam '' (Ah.Chi9/62)

- Sarngadhara samhita : alpaya matraya niruhakhyo basti: pichabasti:
- Indicated in pittaja and raktaja atisara
- Anuvasana – with vilwa tailah or vachadi gana – KV atisara
- Picha vasti –''vata sleshma vibandhe va sravatyati kaphe api va

  sule pravahikayam va picha basti: prashasyate''

- Picha vasti – gudamarga raktapitta, raktarsas

6. sula

- Treatment of Udavarta can be adopted here

- '' udavarta harschasya kriya: sarva sukhavaha:'' (Su.Utt.42
- '' tam taila lavanabhyaktam snigdham swinnam niruhayet

doshato bhinnavarchaskam bhuktam chapi anuvasayet"
(Su.Utt. 55/41)

- According to Susrutha, general line of treatment for Sula is

'' aasukari hi pavanam tasmat tam twaraya jayet
tasya sulabhipannasya sweda eva sukhavaha'' (Su.Utt. 42/)

- Treatment of Sula according to Chakradatta

'' vamanam langhanam sweda: pachanam phalavarttaya:
kshara churnani gulika shasyante sula santhaye"
pumsa sulabhipannasya sweda eva sukhavaha:
Payasei: kiserapindei: snighderva pishitotkarei:'

- in the management of vit sula

'' kshipram dosaharam karyam bhisaja sadhu Janata
swedanam samanam cheiva niruha: snehabastaya: (Su. Utt 42)

- Treatment of gulma also to be adopted here

- ''gulma avastha: kriya: karya yathavat sarva sulinam''(Su.Utt 42)

7. jeerna jwara

- A.c to AH –

''niruhastu balam vahnim vijwaratwam mudam ruchim

doshe yukta: karotyashu pakwe pakwasayam gate pittam va kaphapittam va pakwasaya gatam haret sramsanam treenapi malan vasti: pakwasayasrayan'' here vasti is considered capable of removing all 3 dosa

- Anuvasana is indicated when

'' praksheena kapha pittasya trikaprishta kateegrahe deepta agner badha sakrita: prayunjeetanuvasanam''

- In both niruha and anuvasana, there is specific mentioning of agni. Hence, it can be understood that there is a necessity of confirming the status of agni in a person before administration of Vasti. Other wise it will lead to untoward effects and even deteriorate the patient's condition
- Some yoga used for vasti in jwara – patola nimbadi, chatsra parninyadi, siddha vasti mentioned in kalpa sthana
- according to charaka and chakradatta

'' prayojayet jwaraharan niruhan sanuvasanan pakwasaya gate doshe vakshyante ye cha sidhishu''

- according to susrutha:

'' saruje anilaje karye sa udavarta niruhanam kateeprishta grihartasya deeptagneranuvasanam''

- according to Dalhanan- saruje – koshta ruk yukte sa udavarte- sa vibhandhe

Hence, a clear cut demarcation between the utility of asthapana and anuvasana is mentioned in jwara

when associated with pain in different parts of the body and if there is proper jataragni anuvasana can be done where as When there is a need to remove the morbid matter niruha should be given

8. Pratisyaya

- 2 types – nava and pakwa
- When pratisyaya left untreated – dushta pratisyaya

'' pakwam ghanam chapyavalamba manam
siro vireker apakarshayettam
Virechana asthapana dhoompaner
avekshya doshan kavala graheshcha''(Su.Utt 24)

9. Sukra dosha

- 8 sukra dosha according to Charaka and Susrutha
- General treatment for Sukra dosha according to charaka

''prashasta: sukra dosheshu vastikarma visheshata'' (Cha chi.30/142)

- ''vatanvite hita: sukre niruha sanuvasana:''

- according to Susrutha-

'' snigdham vantam viriktam cha nirudam anuvasitam
yojayet shukra doshartam samyak Uttara vastina''
(Su.Sa.2/10)

10. Vatavyadhi

- In pakwasaya gata vata:

''pakwasayagate cha api deyam Sneha virechanam
vastaya: sodhaneeyascha praschascha lavanottara:''
(Su.Chi4/4)

- In A.Hr- '' vasti karma twadhonabhe: shasyate cha avapeedaka''
- Mamsa meda gata vata- vireko mamsa medasthe niruha: samanani cha (Ah.Chi 21/19)
- In sarvanga vata- ...sarvanga kupite abhyango vastaya: sanuvasana: (Cha.Chi.28/82)
- in avarana chikitsa – pitta avarana –vasti with ksheera madhuraousadha
- kapha avarana – vasti with gomutra

- General treatment of avarana – yapana vasti, anuvasana

- '' sarvasthanavrete apyashu tat karyam marute hitam

yapana vastaya: prayo madhura: sanuvasana:''(Cha.Chi.28/180)

- Relevance of Vasti in Vatavyadhi chikitsa

'' sarvanga gata ekanga sthitam va api sameeranam
runadhi kevalo vastirvayuvegam ivachala:'' (Su.Chi.4/20)

- General line of treatment of vatavyadhi

'' Sneha swedasthatha abhyango basti: Sneha virechanam
sirovasti: sirosneho dhuma snaihika eva ca

sukhoshna: Sneha gandusho nasyam sneihikam eva cha... (Su.Chi.4/26)

- **Vasti in gridhrasi chikitsa**
- according to chakradtta

'' gridhrasyartam naram samyak pachanadhair vishodhitam

njatwa naram pradeeptagnim vastibhi: samupacharet

na aadou vasti vidhim kuryat yavad urdhwam nasuddhyati

sneho nirarthakastasya bhasmanyeva ahutiryatha''

- Placement of vasti – after pachana and with proper agni bala
- Hence, vasti can be effectively used for treatment when proper elimination of urdhwagata dosa has been done.

11. Apasmara & Unmada

- General treatment of Unmada

"unmade vataje poorvam snehapanam visheshavit

...niruham Sneha vastim cha sirasascha virechanam'' (Cha.Chi.9/25)

- **General treatment of Apasmara**

'' teekshneradou bhisakh kuryat karmabhir vamanadibhi:

vatkam vasti bhuyishtei:........ (Cha.Chi 10/14)

- Vasti is considered as the ideal treatment for addressing dosa dusti in pakwasaya.
- But, it is also used for managing psychiatric conditions like unmada and apasmara.
- Thus, the action / utility of vasti is not only on the body but also the mind.
- By creating a pure environment for the body, indriya prasadam and mana prasadam is attained simultaneously.

12. Mutrakrichra, Asmari

''rekartham tailvakam sarpi basti karmam cha seelayeth visheshad Uttara vasti.... (Ah.Chi.11/51)

- Mutrakrichra chikitsa:

''abhyanjana Sneha niruha vasti sweda upanaha Uttaravasti seka

sthiradhibir vataharaischa sidhan dadyat rasamcha anila mutra krichre'' (Chakradatta 32/1)

Mutraghata chikitsa

- '' vastim Uttara vastischa dadyat snigdham virechanam''(Chakradatta.33/1)

in these 2 conditions, Vasti is the general mode of treatment and Uttara vasti is the vishesha chikitsa.

Here mutra marga visodhanam is required, so Uttara vasti is the desired mode.

General practice

- Diseases of musculoskeletal system – multiple joint pain due to OA, LBA

- Peripheral neuropathy – DPN
- Neurological disorders – hemiplegia
- Neurodegenerative diseases – Alzheimer's disease
- Movement disorders – cerebellar ataxia, Parkinson's disease
- Developmental disorders – Cerebral palsy
- Auto immune conditions – RA, SLE, Psoriatic arthropathy
- Gynaecological diseases – infertility, repeated abortions

Basti yoga with indications

- Bala guluchyadi vasti –Ah.Kal4/1-2- brimhanam, vata samanam
- Dwi panchamuladi vasti – Ah.Kal.4/4- sarva anila vyadhi haram
- Lekhana vasti – Su.Chi. 38/82- sthoulyam
- Grahi vasti – Su.Chi. 39/87 – irritable bowel syndrome
- Utkleshana vasti –Su.Chi – 38/93- first among three vasti
- Sodhana vasti – Su.Chi. 38/81 – second vasti
- Samana vasti – su . Chi. 38/95- last among 3 vasti
- Vaitarana vasti – chakradatta – 73/32- sula, anaha, amavatahara
- Ksara vasti – chakradatta – 73/29-31 . Sulam, vitsangam, anaham

contraindications with reason

अनास्थाप्यास्तुअजीर्ण्यतस्निग्धपीतस्नेहोत्क्लष्टिदोषाल्पाग्नि
यानक्लान्तातदिरुबलक्षुत्तृष्णाश्रमार्तातकिश्
भुक्तभक्तपीतोदकवमतिविरिक्तकृतनस्तः-
कर्मकदुध्धभीतमत्तमूर्च्छतिप्रसक्तच्छर्दनिष्ठीवकिाश्वासकासहिक्किा

बद्धच्छिद्रोदकोदराध्मानालसकवसूचिकामप्रजातामातसार-
मधुमेहकुष्ठार्ताः॥१४॥(cha.si.2)

	Disease or State (in which asthapana basti is contraindicated)	Meaning
1	Ajeerna	Indigestion
2	Atisnigdha	Over-unctuous
3	Peetasneha	(A person who has just ingested) smoothening/uncting substances
4	Utklishtha dosha	(A person who has) excited dosha
5	Alpaagni	Suppression of the power of digestion
6	Yaanaklaanta	(A person who is) exhausted due to riding
7	Atidurbala	(A person who is) excessively weak
8	Kshudhaarta	(A person who is) excessively hungry
9	Trishnaarta	(A person who is) excessively thirsty
10	Shramaarta	(A person who is) excessively tired (of doing laborious work)
11	Atikrisha	(A person who is) excessively emaciated
12	Bhuktabhakta	(A person who has) just ingested food
13	Peetodaka	(A person who has) just drunk water

Table 2.1 contraindications of Asthapana basti

14	Vamita	(A person who has) just undergone emesis
15	Virikta	(A person who has) just undergone purgation
16	Krita nastah karma	(A person who has) just used snuff (powder)
17	Kruddha	Anger
18	Bheeta	(A person who is) under the grip of fear
19	Matta	(A person who is) under the influence of narcosis
20	Murchhita	(A person who has) fainted
21	Prasaktachhardi	(A person who is) continuously vomiting
22	Nishtheevika	(A person who is) excessively spitting
23	Shvasa roga	Dyspnea
24	Kaasa roga	Cough
25	Hikka roga	Hiccup
26	Baddhodaraadhmaana	Tympanitis due to intestinal obstruction

Table 2.2 Contraindication of Asthapana basti

27	*Chidrodaraadhmaana*	Tympanitis due to intestinal perforation
28	*Udakodaraadhmaana*	Tympanitis due to ascites
29	*Alasaka roga*	Intestinal torpor
30	*Visuchika roga*	Type of ajeerna avastha
31	*Amaprajaata*	A woman who has delivered a premature baby
32	*Amatisaara*	Diarrhea associated with the symptoms of ama,
33	*Madhumeha*	Diabetes mellitus
34	*Kushtha roga*	Obstinate skin diseases

Table 2.3 Contraindication of Asthapana basti

Adverse effects of asthapana basti administered in contra-indicated persons

तत्राजीर्णयतसि्नग्िधपीतस्नेहानां दूष्योदरं मूर्च्छाश्वयथुर्वा स्यात्, उत्क्लष्िटदोषमन्दाग्न्योररोचकस्तीव्र:,

यानक्लान्तस्य क्षोभव्यापन्नोबस्तरिश् देहं शोषयेत्, अतदिर्बलक्षत्तृष्णाश्रमार्तानां पूर्वोक्तोदोष: स्यात्,

अतकिृशस्य कार्श्यं पुनर्जनयते्,भुक्तभक्तपीतोदकयोर्तुक्लश्ियोर्ध्वमधो वा वायुर्बस्तमित्क्षप्िय क्षप्िरं घोरान् वकिराञ्जनयते्, वमतिवरिक्तियोसत् रूक्ष शरीरं नरिह्ि:क्षत कृषार इव दहते्,

कृतनसत:कर्मणो वभ्िरंशं भृशसंर्दुधसरोतस: कृयात्, क्रूद्धभीतयोर्बस्तरिर्ूध्वमुप्लवते्,

मत्तमूर्च्छतियो र्भृशंवंचिलतियां सञ्ज्ञायां चत्ितोपघाताद् व्यापत् स्यात्,

प्रसक्तच्छर्दरिनिष्ठीवकिश्वासकासहक्किार्तानामूर्ध्वीभूतो वायुर्ूध्वं बस्तनियते्,

बद्धच्छद्रिोदकोदराध्मानार्ताना भृशतरमाध्माप्य बस्ति: प्राणान्
हस्यिात्,

अलसकवसिच्चकिमप्रजातामातसारिणिमामकृतो दोष:स्यात्,

मध्मुहेकष्ुठनिोर्व्याधे: पुन्र्वद्ूध:; तस्मादते नास्थाप्याः॥१५॥
(Cha.Si.2)

Application of Asthapana-basti (non-unctuous enema)
in the persons suffering from indigestion, over-unacted and
just taken unctuous substances causes dushyodara (dare-
roga caused by aggravation of all the three dosha), fainting
or enema. In the cases having excited dosha and
suppression of digestion power, it causes severe type of
anorexia. In a person exhausted due to riding, the
asthapana-basti disturbed by agitation dry up the body
quickly leading to emaciation. In the persons who are
excessively weak and suffering from excessive hunger,
thirst and tiredness, basti causes the same harms as
discussed for exhausted due to riding. In excessively
emaciated person if asthapana-basti is applied, it increases
the emaciation. In those who have just taken food and
water, asthapana basti causes provocation of vat which
divert the enema upwards or downwards leading to
manifestation of severe diseases soon. In that undergone
emesis or purgation, the narwhal or asthapana-basti burns
the body as alkali does the wound. In a person who has
undergone the snuffing, it causes the untoward effects
related to sense organs and further obstruction of the
channels of circulation. In the person having anger and
fear, the basti may go upwards and produce agitation. In the
condition of narcosis and fainting, the basti causes further
agitation and there may be complications due to mental
injury. If asthapana basti is applied in the conditions of
constant vomiting, excessive spitting, dyspnoea, cough and

hiccup, vat moving upwards can cause upward movement of basti. In the persons suffering from intestinal obstruction, intestinal perforation and ascites associated with tympani is, asthapana basti further increase the distension and may lead to the death of the patient. In the persons suffering from Alaska, visuchika, premature delivery and amatisara, it causes the disorders due to ama (product of improper digestion). In diabetes mellitus and kushtha (obstinate skin diseases including leprosy), application of asthapana basti further increases these diseases. Therefore, asthapana basti should not be given to the above mentioned persons

CHAPTER V

Preparation of basti dravya

Ingredients of niruha basti formulation

The main ingredient in niruha basti is a herbal infusion. In addition, it has rock salt, honey, unctuous material (often ghee or oil), and medicinal paste (kalka). Incoterm substitutes for decoction include cow's urine, milk, meat soup, and dhanyamla, a fermented liquid preparation made from grains.

Quantity of ingredients

The following is the general dosage of components for 1152 ml (dvadasha prasruta) basti. The components are combined during production in the precise order and amount specified below:

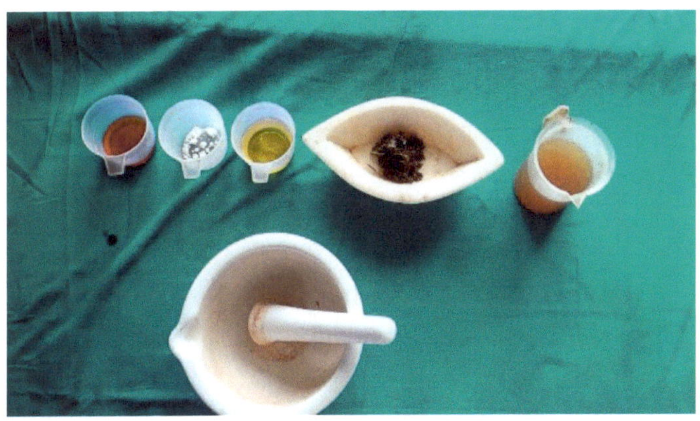

ingredients

1. Honey: 192 ml (2 prasruta)
2. Rock salt (saindhava): 12 gram (1 karsha)
3. Oil/ghee/unctuous substance (sneha): 288 ml (3 prasruta)
4. Medicinal paste (kalka): 96 gram (1 prasruta)
5. Decoction (kwatha): 384 ml (4 prasruta) to 480 ml (5 prasruta)
6. Additives (aavapadravya): 192 ml (2 prasruta)

[Su.Sa.Chikitsa Sthana 38/37-39][Cha.Si 3/30]

Proportion of Sneha dravya and madhu based on dosha predominance

The proportion of sneha dravya and madhu changes based on the predominance of dosha in diseases. It is as shown below in table

Dosha specific proportion in basti formulation

	Vata dosha	Pitta dosha	Kapha dosha
Honey	144 ml (3 pala)	192 ml (4 pala)	288 ml (6 pala)
Unctuous Substance	288 ml (6 pala)	192 ml (4 pala)	144 ml (3 pala)

Table 2 **Dosha specific proportion in basti formulation**

Method of preparation of niruha basti (decoction enema)

The decoction enema is a combination of many ingredients as mentioned above. These ingredients should be mixed in a specific sequence to formulate homogenous mixture and achieve maximum therapeutic efficacy. The sequence of mixing of decoction enema is as follows. Honey and rock salt should be mixed first. Then dravya such as taila or ghrita is added and mixed. Medicinal paste is added next to it and finally the decoction is added.[Cha.Si 3/23] This process acquires the state of emulsion. Due to its medicinal effects and durability, honey is a recommended natural emulsifying ingredient when preparing basti

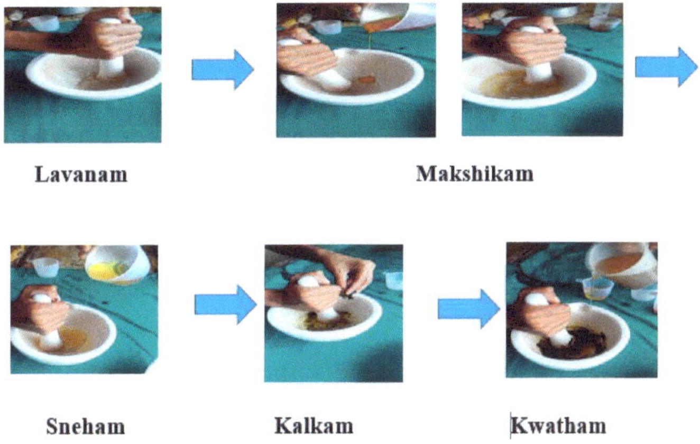

Mixing of Basti ingredients

- **Acc to su chi 38th :**

"datwa adou saindhavakshasyam madhuna: prasrita dwayam
Patre talena mathneeyat tat vat sneham sanei: sanei:
Samyak sumathithe dadyat phala kalkamata: param

Tato yathochitan kalkan bhagei: swei: slakshna peshitaan

Gambheere bhaajane anyasmin mathneeyat tam kajena cha

Yatha va sadhu manyeta na sandro na tanu: sama:
Rasa ksheeramla mutranam doshavasthamavekshya tu
Kashaya prasritan pancha suputamstatra dapayet"

- According to Susruta- saindhava has to be added first.
- Followed by makshikam. Both are mixed well together
- Sneha is added slowly and mixed to create a homogeneous mixture.
- Kalka is added next, Care should be taken not to make thin or thick paste
- It should be of moderate consistency
- The mixing should be done in a large vessel
- Drava appropriate to the vasti should be added
- 5 prasrta of kashaya should be added
- It should be strained well.
- Acc to vagbhata – makshika has to be added first (mangalaartham)
- **Acc to Cha. Si . 3rd –**

''purvam hi dadyat madhu saindhavam cha
Sneham vinirmathya tato anu kalkam
Vimathya samyojya punardraveistam
Vastou nidadhyan mathitham khajena

- **Acc to Ah. Su.**

'' kwathayet vimshatipalam dravyasashtou phalani cha
tata: kwathaat chathurthamsham sneham vate prakalpayet.

pitte swasthe cha sashtamsham ashtamamsam kaphadike

sarvatra cha astamam bhagam kalkat bhavati va yatha

Na atyacha sandrata vaste: pala matram gudasya cha

Madhu patwadi sesham cha yuktya sarvam tat ekata:

Ushnambu kumbhee bashpena taptam khaja samahatam."

- Vasti dravya should be heated indirectly in the vapours of hot water

Features of vasti dravya

"............na atyushna seetalam

Na ati snigdham na va ruksham na ati tikshnam na va mridu

Na atyacha sandram no na atimatram na apatu na ati cha

Lavanam tat vat amlam cha" (Ah.Su. 19th)

improper mixing and their complications (Cha. Si. 3rd (snigdho ati jatyam...)

- If seeta – sthambha
- Ati matram ushnam – murcha, vidaha
- atisnigdha- jadya
- Ruksham- pavana kopa
- Tanu- alpa matra-alavana – ayogam
- Adhikamatra – atiyogam
- Sandra – kshamata, su chiram
- Ati lavana – daha, atisara

Properties of ingredients

1. Makshik (Honey) - It is considered as Auspicious drug. It is having swadu and kashaya rasa, Ruksha Guna

(property) and Ushna Veerya (hot potency). The most important properties of honey in context of Basti Karma are Yogavahitva (synergistic) and Sukshma Marga Anusaritva (potency to penetrate into minute channels of body).It acts as emulsifier which stabilises an emulsion. It is ambiphilic in nature. It has fructose, glucose, sucrose, etc. which get quickly absorbed by digestive system and are converted into energy so acts as instant energizer. It has high nutritive value due to presence of vitamins, minerals, amino acids, fat, etc. It is a very good antioxidant and has simulative effect on colonic probiotic bacteria. It also has specific therapeutic effects like Vrushya (aphrodisiac), Chakshushya (good for eye health), Chedan (excision), Lekhana (scraping).

2. Lavana (salt) - It is salty and mild sweet in taste. It has Laghu (light), Sukshma (minute), Teekshna (sharp), Snigdha (oily) properties and is of Anushna Veerya (not so hot). Owing to its Sukshma characteristic, it can penetrate the body's microchannels. It breaks down the morbid Malas and clears the channels because of its Teekshna virtue. The Dosha is liquefied because of Snigdhaguna. Its irritating quality aids in the removal of the Basti.

3. Dravya. It contains 21 essential and 30 accessory minerals, 98% NaCl and traces of K. It aids in absorption and bio purification action of Basti

4. Sneha - Snigdha Guna produces unctuousness in body which in turn helps in easy elimination of Dosha and Mala (wastes). It pacifies Vata Dosha, softens microchannels and remove obstruction in channels. It shields the mucous membrane in Basti against the negative effects of irritating medications. It aids in the

formation of an emulsion that has healing and cleansing properties.

5. Kalka is the primary medication that provides the entire mixture its strength. By raising the solution's osmotic permeability, it aids in Mala's disintegration. It facilitates the formation of colloidal solutions, expands surface area, and quickens Basti absorption. In addition to other substances, the irritation property has the potential to cause distension in the colon and activate the evacuation reflex.It provides Basti the necessary thickness. It could be Doshahara (extraction), Dosha Shamana (pacification), or Utkleshan (provocation).

6. Kwatha - It increases volume of Basti which in turn lead to increased ability to spread in colon and accelerate absorption of Basti Dravya by increasing surface area. It helps in spreading and cleaning. It helpsin homogenization ofmixture. It has different therapeutic effects. The primary ingredients of Kalka and Kwatha medications are Dosha, Dushya (body tissue), and Srotasa (circulating body channels), which are involved in the pathophysiology of sickness.

7. Avapa - added if the disease is chronic and obstinate

Order of mixing of ingredients

1. The order of mixing has been reported by Acharya Charaka, Vagbhata, and Kashyapa as follows: Makshik, Lavana, Sneha, Kalka, Kwatha, and Avapa

2. The order was given as follows by Acharya Sushruta, Chakradatta, and Vangsena: Saindhav, Madhu, Sneha, Kalka, Avapa, and Kwatha.

Method of mixing of ingredients

Acharya Charaka and Vagbhata has explained the mixing of ingredients with the help of churner. Acharya Sushruta clarified that it must be manually combined in a jar and then blended again till the administration time, after Kashaya has been added. Prior studies have indicated that unidirectional mixing occurs when hand pressure is applied to a mixture while it is being churned. Every particle that travels between the vessel's base and the churner causes the medications to mix well and keep their formulation stable for an extended period of time. Because drug surface area and particle size are inversely correlated, mixing the mixture by hand in a jar will increase its surface area and promote the development of additional collisions.

Thus,the increased surface area exposes drug particles more to the drug media which enhances the rate of reaction. Large surface area exposed to the atmosphere helps in oxidation of active constituents of drug by atmospheric oxygen. According to research done on combining ingredients using a mixer, the ingredients rotate in a single direction around a fixed basis. Moreover, mixer gets heated up while doing the preparation. Hence,the temperature has its impact on final formulation. Separation rate is mild in this method. If mixed with edge runner, it rotates in circular motion with two stands running opposite to each other. This produces both positive and negative mixing, results in union and separation at the same time. Taila and Kwatha split into two layers as soon as they are combined. Particles lose their attraction to one another in this area. Therefore, mixing immiscible materials like Kwatha and Kalka takes a long time. With this procedure, the separation rate is quick. According to one study, the traditional method for preparing basti involves mixing Makshika and Saindhava and continuing to levigate until the sticky sound stops. It was found that the sticky sound disappeared after 30 minutes of levigation. The final product's homogeneity is mostly determined by these two processes. The first two mixing processes determine the success of the subsequent phases, and if they are completed correctly, the remaining two steps don't take longer to create a harmonious mixture. Consequently, each step had a set time of thirty minutes. Basti prepared using a household blender was not stable even for a few seconds, however Basti prepared using a Khalwa (mortar) was stable due to appropriate trituration, according to earlier research. Prior studies have indicated that Basti Dravya can be mixed for ten to fifteen minutes at a period, with a final mixing time of thirty to forty-five minutes. Because the homogenous Basti Dravya is generated and has a longer retention duration than with the usual procedure, Basti Sammilana (formulation) by Hasta Tala (palm of hand) is the ideal way.

A properly prepared basti draya should have the following qualities:

1. It shouldn't flow off and stick to the hand readily.
2. It shouldn't create distinct ingredient layers.
3. It should form a uniform homogenous mixture.

Ayurvedic view behind sequential mixing of ingredients of Basti Acharya Kashyapa has stated that honey being auspicious is first of all poured for the preparation. Salt by its sharpness disintegrates sliminess, denseness and astringentness in honey. These results in compound formation, which is the reason why salt is poured after honey, Then when Sneha is added it brings about uniformity i.e., the contents are properly mixed together.

The Kalka added further gets mingled quickly. The decoction brings about homogeneity. The sharpness and potency are increased by adding urine to this. Additionally, according to Acharya Arundatta, the Basti formulation is homogeneous (Samarasatam Yati) because of the sequential method.

Contemporary perspective on the methodical blending of Basti's components Honey and salt are thoroughly combined to create a stabilizing ingredient called soaping, which provides stability, when making Niruha Basti. Saindhava's sodium aids in the conversion of honey's glucose to hydrogen peroxide.

. Next Sneha should be added because it is a dispersed liquid. It also helps in formation of emulsion. As a result of this Sneha breaking down, short chain free lipids are created, which are quickly absorbed in the small intestine and rectum, especially when Na is present. This is where Saindhava comes in. Unionized and lipid-soluble materials absorb quickly. The mixture is now vigorously churned one more until the stabilizer and dispersed liquid are thoroughly combined. The addition of Kalka should come next since it creates a colloidal solution, expands the surface area, and quickens the absorption of Basti.

Next Kwatha should be added as after adding it the Sneha Dravya gets equally distributed throughout the Kwatha with the help of stabilizer which makes it stable. The mixture thus produced acquire a physical state of emulsion which retains it stable for considerable time. According to the previous research even if all ingredients were added collectively does not affect the end product but after preparation there were lot of bubbles on the surface It may include some oil particles and raise Vata in Basti;

nonetheless, there are no side effects or decreased effectiveness.

1. Kwatha - It increases volume of Basti which in turn lead to increased ability to spread in colon and accelerate absorption of Basti Dravya by increasing surface area. It helps in spreading and cleaning. It helpsin homogenization ofmixture. It has different therapeutic effects. The primary ingredients of Kalka and Kwatha medications are Dosha, Dushya (body tissue), and Srotasa (circulating body channels), which are involved in the pathophysiology of sickness.
2. Avapa - added if the disease is chronic and obstinate

Transfer of medicine to vasti putaka

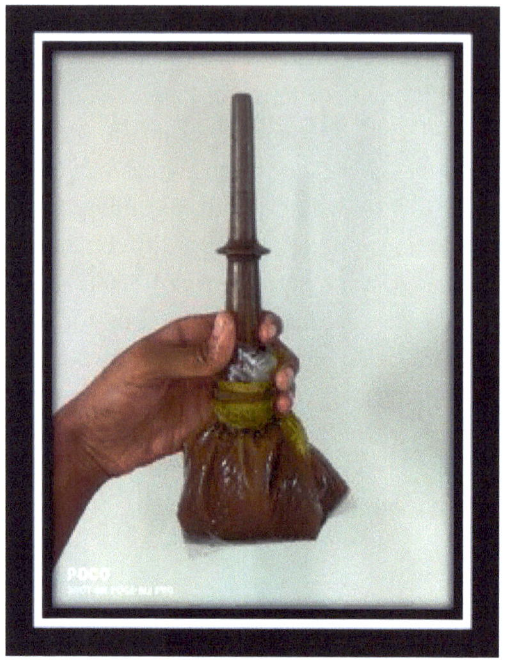

Basti putaka

- **Acc to Susruta**

'' vasatavousadham prakshipya, dakshina hasta angushtena pradeshini madhyamabhyam cha anusiktham anayatam abudbudam asankuchitam avatam ousadhaasannam upasangrihya, punarupari tat itarena griheetwa dakshinena avasinchet, tata: sutreneiva ousadhante dwistriva aaveshty badhneeyat...''

- Medicine should be able to move without obstruction, free of bubbles or air.
- It should be tied to the netra 2/3 times (prevent leakage)
- **Acc to cha.si .3rd**

  ''prakshipya vastou mathitham khajena
  subadham uchwasya cha nrivaleekam
  Angushta madhyena mukham pidhaya
  Netragra samsthamapaneeya vartim''

- Medicine is poured into a putaka devoid of air and wrinkles
- The tip of the vasti netra is plugged using a varti to prevent flow of medicine

CHAPTER VI

Procedure

Therapeutic procedure of administration

- Pre therapeutic procedure (purva karma)
- Therapeutic procedure (pradhana karma)
- Post therapeutic procedure (pashchat karma)

Pre therapeutic procedure (purva karma)
Preparation of patient

- Fixing treatment of patient taking into consideration the *Sameekshya bhava*

  (sameekshya dosha ousadha desha kala
  satmyagni satwadi vayo balani
  vasti prayukto niyatam gunaya
  syat sarva karmani cha sidhimanti cha si 3rd)

- Ascertain patient preparedness on the day of vasti
- Make sure bowel/ urine has been passed
- Sound sleep on the eve of vasti
- Check vitals – BP, Pulse, respiratory rate

  Classical references

- **Acc to cha. Si. 1st**

  '' tailakta gatraya tato niruham
  dadyat trayahat na ati bubhukshitaya''

- **Acc to Cha. Si. 3rd**

  '' aasthapanarham purusham vidhinja:
  sameekshya punye ahni sukla pakshe
  prashasta nakshatra muhurta yoge
  Jeernannamegagram upakrameta''

- ''....tailakta gatram krita mutra vitkam

  Na ati kshudartham sayanemanushyam''

- Acc to hareeta – vasti to be done in krishna paksha
- Reason – sukla paksha is auspicious time – deva jata
- Krishna paska – asura jata- sarva rogascha
- '' tasmat roga chikitsa krishne sadeiva kartavya''
- **Acc to Su Chi .38th :**

  '' atha anuvasitham asthapayet, swabhyakta swinna
  sareera utsrishta bahir vegamavate suchou veshmani...

- Delhana – utsritshta bahirvegam tyakta vinmutradikam
- **Acc to Su. Chi . 38th**

  '' na tu bhuktavate deyam asthapanamiti sthithi:
  Vishuchika va janayet chardim va api sudarunam
  Kopayet sarva doshan va tasmat dadyat abhojine''

- If niruha is given to a person who has consumed food –
  vishuchika, chardi, tridosha kopa

  '' jeernannasya asaye dosha: pumsa: pravayaktimagata:
  ni:sesha: sukhamayanti bhojanena aprapeedita:
  Na va asthapana vikshiptam annam agni: pradhavati

Tasmat asthapanam deyam niraharaya janata"

- **Acc to Ah. Su. 19th**

"abhyakta swedito utsrishta malam na ati bhubhukshitam
avekshya purusham dosha bhesajadeeni chaadraat
vastim prakalpayet tat vidyeir bahubhi: saha"

- Hence patient has to do abhyanga (self), void faeces/ urine, not too hungry and lie down for vasti .
- While charaka emphasized on the need of fixing an auspicious time based on horoscope, Laghu vagbata mentions that maybe more than one experienced physicians will be necessary for the smooth conduct of the procedure.
- **Acc to Sa. Sam. Utt. 6th**

'' utsrishta anila vinmutram snigdha swinnam abhojitam"

- Here the vasti is to be administered in a person who has not taken food.
- **Acc to Vrinda madhava**

'' anuvasitam abhyaktam swinna deham niruhayet abhuktam..

Therapeutic procedure (pradhana karma)

The patient should not be hungry and is encouraged to resist natural cravings on the day of medication. [Sthana Cha.Sa.Siddhi 3/17] The patient's thighs, gluteal area, low back, and abdomen are all massaged locally with oil and sudation. The basti device (basti yantra) is filled with the prepared enema mixture. Two types of basti device are utilized to give decoction enema in clinical practices today.

1. A basti bag with a basti nozzle attached

2. Clear plastic enema jar with catheter and tube attached

The basti bag or enema pot is filled with the enema mixture. After that, a catheter is used to extract the medication's air bubbles.

Therapeutic procedure (pradhana karma)

Patient is asked to lie in left lateral position with left leg extended and right leg flexed at knee and hip.

- **Acc to Cha. Si. 3rd**

''same athava eeshat nnata sheershake va

natyuchrite swastarana upapanne

Savyena parswena sukham sayanam

Kritwariju deham swabhujopadhanam

Sankochya savyetarasya sakthi

Vamam prasarya pranayetat: tam

- Lie comfortably with right knee flexed
- Left leg extended
- Use hand as pillow – folded and kept below head

Significance of position

'vamasraye hi grahani gude cha

Tat parswa samsthasya sukhopalabdhi:

Leeyanta evam valayascha tasmat

Savyam sayano arhati vasti danat'' (Cha.Si. 3rd)

- The grahani and guda vali are situated in the left side.
- Hence, lying on the left lateral position will help in dilation of the sphincters and allow easy upward

movement of vasti ousadha

Administration of medicine

- **Time** – madhyahne / madhyahne kinchit avarte
- The anal orifice and the basti nozzle or catheter are lubricated with oil. Then the basti nozzle is inserted slowly through the anal canal.
- **Direction of insertion of vasti netra**
- Accto cha. Si

'' snigdhe gude netra chaturtha bhaagam
snigdham Sanai: rijvuanu prishtavamsham

- The medicine should be pressed without haste, nor too slow, without shaking.
- It should be squeezed with 1 hand in a single attempt
- If the netra is inserted in tiryak direction – dhara of vasti doesn't occur
- If chalita netra – causes guda vrana
- If given slowly – does not reach asaya
- If given too quickly – kantam pradhavati
- **Acc to Ah. Su. 19th**

Uchwasya vastervadane badhe hastam akamapanam
Prishtavamsam prati tato na ati druta vilambitam
Na ati vegam na va mandam sakrideva prapeedayet
Savasehsam cha kurveeta vayu: seshe hi tishtati''

Niruha peedana kala

- **Time taken to administer the entire vasti dravya**
- The basti bag is squeezed in uniform pressure to pass the basti medicine in rectum.

- Then the nozzle is removed slowly.
- '' tato netram apaneeya trimshanmatra: peedanakalat upekshyottishte ityaturam bruyat''[Cha.Si 3/18-20]
- **Acc to Parasara**

  Time for krura koshta – 100 matra
  madhyama koshta - 70 matra
  mridu koshta – 30 matra

- Vasti pratyagamana kala – 1 muhurtha
- Otherwise – maranam
- ''Agathou parama kalo muhurtho mrithyave param'' (Ah.Su)

To enable enema medication to pass through, the filled enema pot is maintained at a specific height while using the enema pot method. There is a knob on the tube that allows you to adjust the pressure and flow.

After all enema medicine is in the rectum, the patient is advised to lie in supine position till he feels the urge for defecation. When the patient feels the urge, it shall pass. The time duration the administration of medicine and its evacuation is called as retention enema. The decoction enema is expected to come out within 48 minutes after administration. In a study, the retention time of enema with alkali (kshara basti) in maximum number of participants (60%) is reported to be 5 minutes.

Post therapeutic procedure (pashchat karma)

After the evacuation of bowels patient is advised to take hot water bath and light to digest diet based on dominance of dosha as shown below. [Cha.Si 3/27]

Specific diet as per <u>dosha</u>

<u>Dosha</u>	Diet
<u>Vata</u>	Meat soup or green gram soup
<u>Pitta</u>	Milk
<u>Kapha</u>	Soup prepared with cereals (yusha)

Diet after Basti

CHAPTER VII

Important Basti formulations with practical dosage

Basti formulations described in this chapter are :-

1. Balaguduchyadi basti
2. Dwipanchamuldi basti
3. Balapatoladi basti
4. Erandamuladi basti
5. Yapana basti- mustadi raja yapana basti, madhutailika basti,
   siddhabasti
6. Vaitarana basti
7. Kshara basti
8. Mutra basti
9. Ksheera basti
10.vatahara basti
11. pittahara basti
12. Kaphahara basti

Bala guluchyadi basti

"बलांगुडूच्चींत्रफिलांसरास्त्रादंद्वपिञ्चमूलंचपलोन्मतिानअिष्ट
फलान्यर्धतुलांचमांसाच्छागात्पचेदप्सञ्चत्रूथशेषम् १
पूतोयवानीफलबलि्वकष्ठ - वचाशताहुनाघनपपि्पलीनाम
कल्कैर्गुडुक्षौद्रघतृ:सतैलैर्युक्त:सुखोष्णोलवणान्वतिश्च
बस्तिः:परसंर्वगदपरमाथीस्वस्थेहतिोजीवनबहृणश्च "(A.H K ¼)

Ingredients	quantity
madhu	200ml
Saindhavam	15gm
Taila	150ml
Guda	150ml
Ghritha	400ml
Kashaya- Bala, guduchi, triphala, rasna ,dasamula- 1 pala each, 8 madana & ½ thulam chagamamsa	Mamsarasa-200ml
Kalka-yavani phala vilwa etc-	30gm (1100)

Practical dosage

- Based on yukti, oil or ghee can be changed.
- If both are added, they are taken equally.
- For mamsarasa goat meat is used.

As per Dalhana - mamsarasa should be 16 pala

Arunadatta- kalka- 2 pala

In Vata, Pitta, Kapha – sneha- 1/4, 1/6, 1/8 of total quantity

In context, where kalkadravya is not mentioned, this yavanyadi kalka is used.

- Indications : sarvaroga ,can be used for swastha, jeevana, brimhana

Dwipanchamuladi basti

द्वपिञ्चमूलस्यरसऽम्लयुक्त:सच्छागमांसस्यसपूर्वपेष्य
त्रसिनेहयुक्त:प्रवरोनरिह्:सर्वानलिव्याधहिर:प्रदष्टि:४

(Ah k 4/4)

Ingredients	quantity
Madhu	200ml
Saindhavam	15gm (7.5)
Sneha- trisneha (sarpi, majja, vasa- Sa Su)	300ml (eranda-50, ghritha-50, taila-50)
Kalka - yavanyadi	30gm
Kwatha – dasamula, chagamamsa, amladravya	200ml+200ml+200ml (600+75+75ml)

Practical dosage

- Indication : all vatavyadhi

Balapatoladi basti

बलापटोलीलघुपञ्चमूल त्रायन्तकिरैण्डयवात्सुसद्धिात् पुरस्थो रसाच्छागरसार्धयुक्तः साध्यः पुनः पुरस्थसमः स यावत् ५ पुरयिङ्गुकृष्णाघनकल्कयुक्तः सतैलसर्पर्मिधुसुनैन्धवश्चस्याद्दीपनो मांसबलपुरदश्च चक्षुरूबलं चोपदधार्तासद्यः ६ (Ah k 4/4)

Ingredients	quantity
Madhu	200 ml
Lavanam	15gm
Sneham (taila+ghrita)	300ml -taila+ghrita (50taila)
Kalkam- priyangu, krushna, Ghana	30gm
Kwatham- bala patolam laghupanchamula, trayanti, eranda , yava	400ml
Mamsarasa	200ml (mamsarasa)

Practical dosage

- Indications : mamsa bala prada ,deepana,chakshushya,

GB Syndrome, muscular dystrophy,macular atrophy

Erandamuladi basti

एरण्डमूलात्रपिलंपंलाशात्तथापलांशंलंघुपञ्चमूलम
रास्नाबलाछन्निरुहाश्वगन्धापुनर्नवारग्वधदवेदार्
फलानचिष्टौसलललिढकाभ्यांवपिाचयदेष्टमशेषेतिऽस्मनि
वचाशताहुलाहपुष्पापुरयिड्गयष्टीकरणावत्सकबीजमसुतम्
दद्यात्सुपुष्टिसंहतार्यशैलमक्षपुरमाणंलवणांशयुक्तम
समाक्षकिसुतैलयुसमूतूरोबस्तरिजयेल्लेखनदीपनोऽस
जङ्घोरुपादत्ररकिपृष्ठकोष्ठहृद्गुह्यशूलंगुरुतांवबिन्धम
गुल्माश्मवर्ध्यगुरहणीगुद्रोत्थांस्तांस्तांश्चरोगान्कफवातजातान्१०(Ah
k 4/7)

Ingredients	quantity(N
Madhu	200
Lavanam	15
Sneham	200
Kalkam- vacha, satahwa, hapusha, priyangu,yashti, kana, vatsakabeejam, mustam	30
Kashaya- erandamulam, palasam 3palam each, laghupanchamulam , rasna bala chinnaruha aswagandha, punarnava, aragwadha devatharu, 8 madana	600ml
Gomutra-	75ml

Practical dosage

YAPANA BASTI

- Aayusho yaapanam deerghakaalaanuvartanam kurvanti iti yapanaa vastaya: (Ca si 12/15-cakra)
- Yapanam- prolonging or supporting the life
- 216 yogas in Caraka Sidhi stana- 29 are original yogas, 187 are extended yogas
- Swathaanaam aturaanaam cha vrudhaanaam cha avirodhina.... (Ca si 12/20)

Benefits

- Sukramamsabalaprada
- Sarvarogaprasamana
- Sarvartushu yougika
- Apatyada
- Ubhayarthakara ishta snehabasti niruhayo:
- having particular action on sukradhatu- vrushya
- **composition**

- Saindhavam, madhu, kashaya , ksheera, mamsarasa, eggs, ghrita, guda etc
- Only murchita tailam is used
- Most of them – padahina basti unless specified quantity is mentioned

A) Mustadi yapanabasti (Ah K 4/ 37, ca si 12/16-1)

मुस्तापाठाऽमृतैरैण्डबलारास्त्राप्नुनर्नवाः,
मञ्जष्ठिारग्वधोशीरत्रायमाणाक्षरोहिणीः३
कनीयःपञ्चमूलंचपालकिंमदनाष्टकम्
जलाढकेन पचेत्तच्चपादशेषंपरसिरुतम्३८
क्षीरद्वपिरस्थसंयुक्तंक्षीरशेषंपुनःपचेत्
सपादजाङ्गलरसःससर्पर्मिधुसुनैन्धवः३६
पष्टिरै्यष्टमिसिशिग्यामाकलङ्गिकरसाञ्जनैः
बस्तःसुखोष्णोमांसाग्नबिलशकु्रवविरुद्धनः४०
वातासङ्ग्मोहमहार्शोगुल्मवटि् मूत्ररसङ्ग्रहान्
वषिमज्वरवीसरपवरत्माध्मानपुरवाहकिाः४१
वङ्क्षृणोरु्कटीकुक्षमिन्याश्रोत्रशरीरुजः
हन्यादसगृदरोन्मादशोफकासाश्मकुण्डलान्४२
चक्षुष्यःपुतुरदोराजायापनानारंसायनम्

- Kashaya- musta, pata, amrutha eranda bala rasna punarnava manjishta aragwadha useera, trayamana aksharohini, lahghupanchamulam- 1 pala each& 8 madana- in jaladhake – reduced to ¼
- 2 prastha ksheera- ksheerakashaya
- Mamsarasa- ¼ of niruha (6pala)
- Ghee, honey, saindhava
- Kalka- yasti misi syama kalingaka rasanjana

Contents	Quantity
Saindhava	15g
Madhu	100 ml
Taila	50 ml
Ghrita	50 ml
Kalka	30g
Ksheera kashaya	240ml
Mamsa rasa	100

Practical dosage

B)Madhu tailika basti

मधुतैलेसमेकर्ष:सैन्धवाद्द्वपिचिरुमसिि:||२७||

एरण्डमूलक्वाथेननरिह्होमाधुतैलकि:|

रसायनंप्ंरमहार्श:कृमगिलुमान्त्रवद्धधनितु||२८||

सयष्टमिधुक्रश्चचैषचक्षुषुयोरक्तपत्तिजति्|

(Ah K 4/27)

Ingredients	Quantity
Madhu	120 ml
Taila	120 ml
Erandamula Kashaya	480 ml
Saindhava	15 g

practical dosage

- Saindhavam- karsham
- Satakuppa- 2karsham
- Yasmaat madhu cha tailam cha pradhanyena atra varthate

"Madhutailikam ithyesham bhishagbhi: bastiruchyathe"
(su ci 38/114)

- **Ca Si 12/18 (13)**
- Madhu tailam chatu prasrutam satapushpardhapalam saindhava ardhaakshayukto basti: deepano brumhano balavarnakaro nirupadrava vrushyatamo rasayana: krumikoshta udaavarta gulma arso bradhna pleeha mehahara

<u>Characteristics of madhutailika basti</u>
"Nrunaam tat samaanaanam tathaa sumahataamapi
Nareenam sukumaraanaam sisusthavirayorapi
Doshanirharanaarthaaya balavarnodayaaya cha
Samasena upadekshyaami vidhaanam maadhuailikam
Yaanastreebhojyapaaneshu niyamascha atra na uchyate
Phalam cha vipulam drushtam vyaapadam cha api asambhava:
Yojyastwata: sukhenaiva niruhakramamichataa
Yadechati tadevaisha prayoktavyo vipaschitaa" (Su Ci 38/96)
<u>Suitable for :</u>
sukhinam alpadoshanam nityam snigdhascha ye naraa:
Mrudukoshtaascha ye thesham vidheya madhutailika: (Su Ci)

- 2 types – with erandamula kwatham- need anuvasana

  with milk/mamsarasa no need of anuvasana

- **Maddhutailika viseshavidhi- Ah k 4/28 – Chakshusya basti**

"Sa yashtimadhukascha esha chakshushyo raktapittajit" - when Yashtimadhu is added it become chakshya and beneficial in raktapitta.

<u>According to sharngadhara</u>

Erandakwatha thulyamsam madhu tailam palaamsakam

Satapushpa palaardhena saindhavardhena samyutham

Madhutailakaamnjo ayam basti: khajaviloditha:

Medo gulma krumi pleeha malodaavarta naasana :

Balavarnakaraschaiva vrushyo deepana brumhana : (Sa Sam u 6/29-31)

<u>Acc to sar sam u 6/25-28</u>

• Dosha	• Madhu (pala)	• Sneha (pala)
• Vata	• 4	• 6
• Pitha	• 4	• 3
• Kapha	• 6	• 4

Quantity of madhu and sneha according to dosha

C)yuktarathabasti

- Ratheshu api cha yukteshu ityaswe cha api kalpithe

Yasmat na pratishiddho ayam ato yuktaratha: smruta:
(su ci 38/115)

- Erandamula nishkwathe madhu tailam sasaindhavam

Esha yuktaratho basti : savachapippaliphala
(sar sam u 6/33)

- Vachamadhukatailam cha kwatho sarasa saindhava:

Pippaliphalasamyuktho basti yuktaratha: smruta:
(Su ci 38/102)
D)Siddhabasti

- Useful for curing many diseases
- **Yasmin vastou yatha yukte dhruva siddhi: prakeertitaa**

Sidhabastiriti khyaato munibhi: tatwadarshibhi:

- .. Sarvadaa tan prayojayeth

Nirvyapado bahuphalaan balapushtikaraan sukhaan (Ah k 4/26)

- Balopachaya varnaanam yasmaat vyadhisatasya cha

Bhavatyetena siddhistu siddhabastirato mata: (Su ci 38/ 116)

- <u>**No restrictions in siddhabasti because :-**</u>
- Mrudutwat padaheenatwat akrutsna vidhi sevanaat

Ekabastipraadaanat cha siddhabastishu ayantrana (Su ci)

- Panchamulasya nishkwatha: tailam magadhika madhu

Sasaindhava samadhuka: sidhabastiriti smrutha: (Sa Sam)

Siddhabasti I (Sa Sam U 6/33)

"Erandamula nishkwathe madhu tailam sasaindhavam

Esha yuktaratho basti : savachapippaliphala"(sar sam u 6/33)

- Tridoshahara in nature
- synonym of madhutailika
- So indications are same as that of madhutailika
- High safety profile.

Ingredients	Quantity
Madhu	200 ml
Lavana	15g
Sneha	200ml
Kalka	30g
Kashaya	400 ml

practical dosage - sidhabasti

Siddhabasti 2 (VS 83/177)

- Gomutra- 8 pala
- Guda, amlavetas- 1 pala each
- Kalka- satahwa- 1 karsha

- Saindhava- 1 karsha
- given as ruksha in amavata
- And adding Taila- 1 pala in udavarte vatakoshte

Ashtanga sangraha

- Snigdhabasti instead of siddhabasti
- It denotes the predominant oily nature and the prolonged usage like that of matrabasti.
- it should not be confused with anuvasana

Yapana basti- VS 83/176

- Madhu- 1 prasruta
- Ghrita- 1 prasruta
- Ksheera- 1 prasruta
- Taila - 1 prasruta
- Kalka- hapusha- 1 karsha
- Saindhava- 1 karsha
- Yapana: para
- Excessive use of yapana – adverse effects

Sopha agninasa pandutwa sula arsa parikarthikaa:
Syu: jwarascha atisaarascha yapana atyarthasevanaat
(ca si 12/30)

- Management

"Arishtaksheera seedhvadya tatreshta deepani kriya"
Vaitarana basti (CD 73/32)
पलशकृत्तकिरूषकडुवैरम्लीगुडसन्धिज्जन्ममोमूत्रैः।
तैलयुतोऽयंवसुतः शूलानाहामवातहरः॥

वैतरणःक्षारवस्तर्भुक्तेचापप्रिदीयतो।।
इतविैतरणवस्तिः।। (चक्रदत्त, नरि्हाधकिारः३)

- Amlika- 1 pala
- Guda-1 sukti
- Sindhujanma- 1 karsha
- Gomutra- 1 kudava
- Tailam- 1 kutavam
- Sula anaha amavatahara---bhukte chaapi pradeeyathe

Vangasena samhita

"Sindhudhwasya   karsham   amleekaya: palam gudardhapalam

Surabhipaya: kudava: sarvai: ethai: kruto basti:

Eeshat tailayuto ayam bhukte date nihanti rogaganam

Kati uru prushta sodham sulam cha amaanilam ghoram

Chiramavamurustambham   gridhrasirogam   cha jaanusankocham

Vishamajwaraani ghoram klaibyascha vinaasataayasu

Bastirvaitaranokto gunaganayukta: suvikhyaata:

Bhojayitwaa cha sayahne sarvasyaayam prasasyate

Atha   chet   balavaan   janthu: abhuktwaapi   tadaa kwachit"(VS)

- saindhava-karsham
- Amlika- 1pala
- Guda-1/2 pala, eeshat taila
- Surabhipaya:--1 kudava

Ingredients	Quantity
Saindhava	15g
Gudam	30g
Taila	120ml
Amlika	60g
Gomutra	240ml

Vaitarana basti- practical dosage

- Indications - Lekhana; katigraha, sula, anaha, amavata are the indns.
- Vaitarana is the name of river which a person is supposed to cross during death in his astral realm. This basti is so powerful in a sense that it can bring back life of a person who is about to cross the vaitarana river. It is told by chakradatta and vangasena. It Can be administered even after the meal. The word surabhipaya: can be interpreted as milk or urine of cow. Based on the need either of these can be selected. Jaggery is added with hot water and melted, filtered and mixed like honey.Tamarind is the kalka used here. If we want to add milk, very hot milk cant be used , and mix very slowly by adding little by little, so that the spoiling of milk will be prevented. Mixing take double the time than other bastis.

- **Kshara basti (CD 73/34), VS**
- The term kashara indicates kshapana karma not ingredient as kshara

"सैन्धवाक्षसंमदायशतावाक्षतंथैवच।
गोमूत्ररस्यद्वेपलान्यष्टावलकिायाःपलद्वयम्।।
गुडस्यद्वेपलेचैवसर्वमालोडययत्नतः।
वस्त्रपूतंसुखोष्णनन्चबस्तर्दिध्याद्वचिक्षणः॥
शूलंवटिसगंमानाहंमूत्रकर्च्छरचदारुणम्।
क्रमिघ्द्वावर्तगुल्मादीन्सद्योहन्यन्नषिवतिः।   Chakradatta,
Vangasena

Saindhava - 1karsham

Guda- 2 pala

Satakuppa- 1 karsham

Amlika 2pala

Gomutram- 8pala

Ingredients	Quantity
Saindhava	12g
Guda	120g
Satapushpa	12g
Amlika	120g
Gomutra	480ml

Kshara basti-practical dosage

Indications : Sulam, vitsangam, anaham, mutrakruchram cha darunam,Krimi, udavarta, gulma

Also useful in Amavata,adhmana,arsas,shula, sthoulya, prameha

Anuvasanam needed- before and after

Mutrabasti (VS 83/182)

- Gomutra- 8 pala
- Eranda Kwatha- 4 pala
- Taila-2pala
- Madhu- 2 pala

- Mamasarasa, kshira, souvira, amlika- 1 pala each
- Guda, madana- 1pala each
- Satakuppa, vacha, rasna, kushta, daru, Ghana, nisa, sarshapa, vilwa,yavani, bala, saindhava- 1 karsha each

Ingredients	Quantity
Gomutra	400ml
Eranda kwatha	200ml
Taila	100ml
Madhu	100ml
Mamsa rasa,ksheera,souveera,amlika	50g each
Kalka	15g
Guda,madana phala	50g each

Practical dosage

- Indications : Nirapaayam mahatgunam, sarvavyadhihara: para:

Ksheerabasti

"Ksheerat dwou prasrutou karyou madhutailaghritaastraya:

Khajena mathito basti: vataghno balavarnakrut"

(Ah K 4/21)/ Ca si 8

ksheera- 2 prasrutha

Madhu- 1 prasruta

Taila- 1 prasruta

Ghrita- 1 prasruta

Contents	Quantity
Madhu	120 ml
Taila	120ml
Ghrita	120 ml
Ksheera kashaya	240 ml bala, aswagandha, madhuka- each 10g- 240ml milk, 960ml water

ksheerabasti - practical dosage

Vatahara basti

- Su ci 38/77

- Kashaya- vataghnoushadha -8pala (dal.)
- Saindhava- 3 tanka
- Traivrita sneha- 6pala
- Amla (ksheera by dal.)
- Sukhoshna basti

- AH K 4

- 1. Balaguluchyadi basti
- 2. dwipanchamuladi basti
- 3. ksheerabasti
- 4. taila, prasanna, madhu, sarpi -1pala each

brihat panchamula kashaya +kulatha kashaya- 2 prasruta each

Pittahara basti

- Su Ci 38/78

- Nyagrodhadi gana ks.- 8pala
- kalka-(3 pala)-Kakolyadi 2pala +Sarkara 1pala
- Ghritha- 4pala
- Ikshurasa- 1pala

- AH K 4

- 1. yashtyahwadi
- 2. Rasnavrushaadi basti

Kaphahara basti

- Su Ci 38/79

- Kashaya- aragwadhadi- 8pala
- Kalka- pippalyadi – 3pala
- Madhu- 6pala
- Saindhava- 3 tanka
- Katutaila-3 pala
- Mutra-3 pala and 7 tanka

- AH K 4

- 1. kosatakyadi (Ah K4/17)
- Kapharoga, mandagni, annadweshi

Pichha basti

अशान्तावत्यियतीसारेपच्छिाबस्तःपरंहंतिः७२
परविष्ट्यकुशुरैरार्थैरार्द्रवनृतानशाल्मलेः
कृष्णमृत्तकियाऽलपियस्वदेयदेगोमयाग्ननिा७३
मृच्छोषेतानसिङ्क्षुद्यतत्पणिडंमुष्टसिम्मतिम्
मर्दयत्पयसःपूरस्थेपूतेनास्थापयेत्ततः७४

नतयष्ट्याह्नकल्काज्यक्षौद्रतैलवताऽन्नु
सुनातोभुञ्जीतपयसाजाङ्गलेनरसेनवा७५
पत्तितातसिरज्वरशोफगुल्मसमीरणास्रग्रहणीविकिरान्
जयत्ययंशीघ्रमतप्रिवृत्तर्विरिचनास्थापनयोश्चबस्तः७६(A.Hr chikitsa)

<u>Susruta</u>

- ksheeraKashaya-ankura of badari, nagabala, naruvari, salmali, dhanwana
- Blood of varaha/ mahisha etc
- Madhu- 200ml
- Lavana- 15g
- Sneha : nalpamaradi kera-100ml

Charngeryadi ghrita- 100ml

- Kalka-30g
- Kashaya- 350ml
- (750ml) (PPV)
- In VS, instead of badari, vidari kanda is mentioned
- **Different piccha basti formulations**

1.

- Madhu- 100ml
- Taila- 100ml
- Ghrita- 100ml
- Kalka- nata & madhuka- 30g
- Putapakadrava of salmali-400ml

2.

- Sugar- 8g
- Madhu- 50ml
- Ghrita- 50ml
- Kalka- 28g (narumpasa, chandana, njazhal poovu, tamarayalli, padarchunda veru, chengazhi, kutakapalayari- each 4gm)
- Kshira kashaya- 600ml –(roots of kodithuva, ama, kusa, ilavin poovu, peral mottu, arrayal mottu, athi mottu- 420g in 600ml milk and 2 L water)

Contents	Quantity
Madhu	100ml
Taila	100ml
Ghrita	100ml
Kalkam	30g
Putapaka drava	400ml

Practical dosage

Indications : pitta atisara,jwara,shopha,gulma

CHAPTER VIII

Anuvasana basti

According to Acharya Sushruta, Anuvasana is a type of Snaihika Basti which is prepared with requisite amount and properties and in quantity less than Niruha Basti in three quarters. Anuvasana is so called as it is not harmful even if staying in body or it is applied daily.

Etymology

- Anu + vaasa – sourabhye lyuta
- Anuvasati , anuvaasaram deeyate va (vachaspatyam)

Definition

- Yatascha so annam anuvasannapi na dooshyati anuvaasaramapi va deeyata ityanuvasanam (AS Su 28/9)
- Yataschaasou anuvasannapi na dushyati, anuvaasanamapi va deeyate ityanuvasanam . Vaasanam-bhojanam (hemadri about AS)
- Anuvasanam yadharhoushadha siddha: snehanartha: sneha:(As su 28/7)
- Anuvasannapi na dushyati anudivasam va deeyata ithyanuvasana: (Su Ci 35/18)
- Indu- yastu vasti: snehanartham yatha dosham yatha vyadhi cha oushadhai: siddha: sneho deeyate tadanuvasanam-ie vasti using sneha prepared with medicines acc to dosha and vyadhi is k as anuvasana

Classification

- Based on Matra

1. sreshta matra –6 pala (Del- tantrantare)

madhyama matra –3pala

kaneeya matra - 1 ½ pala

It is explained by delhana as the opinion of other acharyas that "Shatpalee thu bhavet sreshta madhyama tripalee bhavet

Kaneeyasya adhyardhapala tridha matra anuvasane "

Gayi thu "yathapramaana vihithaascha vaste: padamsa: snehavasti, snehavikalpo ardhamaatraapakrushto anuvasanam, tasyaapi vikalpo ardhamatra apakrushto apariharyo matravastirithi"

2. Snehavasti- 6 pala(Gayadasa)

Anuvasana – 3 pala

Matravasti – 1 ½ pala

3. Constant dose & Escalating dose

Useful dravya

Acharya Charaka has mentioned Anuvasanopaga Gana which consists of following 10 Dravayas.

1. Rasna - Pluchea lanceolata

2. Suradaru - Cedrus deodara

3. Bilva - Aegle marmelos

4. Madanaphala - Randia dumetorum

5. Shatapushpa - Anathem sowa

6. Vrischira - Boerhavia diffusa

7. Punarnava - Trianthema portulacastrum

8. Shwadanshtra - Tribulus terrestris

9. Agnimantha - Premna integrifolia

10. Shyonaka - Oroxylum indicum

Additionally, Acharya Charaka suggested Patala, Agnimantha, and other Dravyas in Sutra Sthana that can be employed for Aasthapana Basti. It has also been mentioned that when these Dravyas are used along with Sneha, the action of Anuvasana Basti occurs.

Indications of Anuvasana Basti

- "Asthapya : eva cha anuvasya visheshat ati vahnaya:

  ruksha kevala vatartha...............(Ah.Su.19/6-7)

- "ya eva asthapyastha evanuvasya:, visheshatastu ruksha teekshnagnaya: kevala vata rogartascha; eteshu hyanuvasanam pradhanatamam ityuktam mule drumaprasekavat" (Ca si 2/19)
- "tatha jwaratisara timira pratisyaya siroroga adhimandha ardita akshepaka pakshaghata ekanga sarvanga roga adhmanodara yonisula sarkarasula vrudhi upadamsa anaha mutrakrichra gulma vatasonita vatamutrapureesha udavarta sukrartava sthanyanasa hrut hanu manyagraha sarkarasmari mudagarbhaprabhrutishu cha atyartham upayujyate" (Su ci 35/4)

<u>Daily anuvasana</u>

"Rukshanityastu deeptagni: vyayami marutaamayi Vamkshana sroni udavrutta vatascharha dine dine"

- ....anyesham tryahaat praya: sneham pachati pavaka: (Ca Si 5/46)

The situations and Vyadhis in which Anuvasana Basti can be administered have been stated by ancient Acharyas. These include:

1. Any condition for which Niruha Basti is recommended.

2. A person with Tikshna Agni and Ruksha, which indicate a healthy digestive system.

3. A person with Kevala Vatavyadhi, or the absence of Aama connection.

Contraindications and Adverse Effects

...Naanuvasya tha eva cha

Ye na asthapya: tatha pandu kamila meha peenasa:

Niranna pleeha vidbhedi gurukoshta kaphodara:

Abhishyandi krusa sthula krumikoshta adyamaruthaa:

Peethe gare vishe apachyam sleepadi galagandavan **(Ah su 19/7-8)**

Acharya Charaka has enlisted the conditions and Vyadhis where Anuvasana Basti should not be administered. When Anuvasana Basti is used in these circumstances without proper recognition, there might be severe negative consequences.

Contraindications - Adverse effects

Abhuktabhakta Avastha- Anuvasana Basti moves upwards due to the absence of any obstruction in Annavaha Srotasa

Nava Jwara, Kamala, Pandu, Prameha- Doshotklesha leading to manifestation of Udararoga

Arshas- Abhhishyanda in Arsha and Aadhmana

Arochaka-Further impaired desire of food

Mandagni, Durbala Agni- Further weakening of Agni that is digestive power

Pratishyaya, Pleeha, Kahodara, Urustambha, Varchobheda, ingestion of Visha as well as Gara, Pittaja Abhishyanda, Kaphaja Abhishyanda, Guru Koshtha, Shleepada, Galaganda, Apachi, Krimikoshtha- Excessive aggravation of already excited Doshas

Ratrau (In the night)- Doshotklesha, Aadhmana, Gaurava, Jwara

Day time in Ushna Kala and Pittadhikya-daha
After intake of Ruksha Aahara-Bala and Varna nasha
After intake of Atisnigdha Aahara-Mada and Murccha
Time of administration

- "...sada anuvasayet cha api bhojayitwa ardrapaninam"...(Su Ci37/53)
- 9th day after virechana, - on 9th day after virechana karma
- 'sadya:' after niruha – immediately after niruha karma
- "Niruha sodhitan margaat samyaksneho anugachati

Apeta sarvadoshaasu nadeeshu iva vahat jalam .....(Su Ci 35/20)

By niruha the srotas become clear and through that srothas, sneha will reach everywhere like water flowing through clear channels. Vasti can act as sarvadoshahara and jeevana , so snehavasti should be given only after visudhadeha (after kashayavasti)

- **Seete vasanthe diva, ratrou kechit thatho anyatha** (Ah su 19/21,)

In seeta and vasanta rutu – anuvasana should be done in day time, in sarat-greeshma-ghanagama ; should be done in ratry

- Ashtanga Sangraha, Indu- *"...athava doshadushya athuradeenavekshya ratrou diva va"* ; can be done in diva or ratri according to the patient condition
- Sushruta- *ratrou vasti na dadyat thu doshotkleso hi ratrija:* -contraindicated in night due to chances of utklesha and produce adhmanam, gouravam , jwaram. But In

conditions like pithe adhike, kaphe ksheene , ruksha and extreme vatakopa, - anuvasana should be given at night.

<u>Pradhana karma</u>

Anuvasana Basti Vidhi

The complete protocol for the governance of Anuvasana Basti has been articulated by ancient Acharyas. Purva Karma, Pradhana Karma, and Paschata Karma are the three categories.

Purva Karma

Examination of patient:

By examining the patient for Dosha, Aushadha, Desha, Kala, Satmya, Agni, Satva, Vaya and Bala, appropriate type of Basti and Basti Dravyas should be selected.

Required equipment:

The development of devices for administering Basti has simplified its application. Because of this, Basti Dravya can be given under complete aseptic precautions instead of Basti of different animals and Basti Netra with the aid of a 100ml glycerine syringe, a straightforward rubber catheter, and hand gloves.

How to make Basti Dravya:

Medicated oil made with amla and vataghna dravyas should be used for Anuvasana Basti. For simple Pratyagamana, mix it with Shatapushpa and Saindhava Lavana. Neither too much heat nor cold is ideal. Because the use of Aamataila may produce Abhishyanda in Guda, it should be prepared carefully.

Preparation of patient

i. Snehana and Swedana: Patient should be massaged well and Swedana with hot water should also be done.

ii. Diet: After this, patient should be fed with Yusha, Kshira and Mansarasa in Kaphaja, Pittaja and Vataja Vikara respectively. The quantity of food consumed should be a quarter that of the typical diet.

iii. Chankramanadi: Now, the patient should be asked to walk few steps and to pass faeces and urine.

Pradhana Karma

This comprises of administration of Basti Dravya after positioning of the patient and observations of Lakshanas for Samyaka Yoga, Ayoga,atiyoga

Position- Patient should be made in left lying down position. Given that Grahani and Guda are situated on the left side of the body, this posture aids in achieving the desired outcomes. Additionally, this maintains the sphincters' immersion in the surrounding muscle.

The prepared Basti Dravya should be administered in this foresaid position and after this, buttocks of the patient should be tapped with the palms to prevent the early return of the oil from the anus. The patient should lie on the bed in supine position and toes of both legs should be pulled gently. His both soles as well as heels, toes, calf regions and other painful parts should be massaged with oil. After this, the patient should sleep comfortably by keeping his head over a pillow and should avoid any other work. Acharya Sushruta has suggested that patient should be made to lie in the supine position till hundred Matra that is till pronouncing of a short vowel hundred times. It has been also suggested that palms, soles and buttocks should be struck slowly three times each and then the cot should be raised up three times.After this, observation of Lakshanas should be done.

Samyak – Ayoga – Atiyoga Lakshana

Anuvasana Basti Samyaka Yoga Lakshana Proper administration of Anuvasana Basti results in following signs and symptoms.

1. Pratyetyasakti tailam sashakriccha (Return of Bastidravya that is medicated oil with fecal matter without any obstruction)

2. Raktadi Prasada (Purity of Rasa-Raktadi Sapta Dhatu)

3. Buddhi and Indriya Prasada (Clarity of intellect and sensory organs)

4. Swapnanuvritti (Calm and continuous sleep)

5. Laghuta and Bala (Lightness and strength to the body)

6. Srishtavega (Proper manifestation of natural urges without any obstruction)

Acharya Sushruta suggested that when Anuvasana Basti returns soon with Vata and Purisha without causing heat and sucking pain then it should be considered as its SamyakaYoga.

Basti Anuvasana Lakshanas Ayoga When Anuvasana Basti is applied improperly, the following symptoms and indicators appear. 1. Ruk (pain in the lower body, abdomen, arms, back, and sides of the body) in Adhosharira, Udara, Bahu, Prishtha, and Parshva 2. The Ruksha and Khara Gatrata (body roughness and dryness) 3. Graha of Vit, Mutra, and Samira (blockage in the flatus, urine, and stool pathways) Basti Anuvasana Lakshanas Atiyoga Anuvasana Basti overuse can lead to Hrillasa (vomiting), Moha (difficulty concentrating), Klama (mental weariness), Sada (tiredness), Murccha (passing out), and Vikartika (pain that grips).

Acharya Vagbhata mentioned that Samyaka Yoga, Ayoga and Atiyoga Lakshanas of Anuvasana Basti are same as that of Snehapana.

Paschata Karma:

After the administration of Anuvasana Basti Dravya, following points should be focused –

1. Basti Pratyagamana Kala

2. Pathya and administration of other Basti

Basti Pratyagamana Kala:

The Anuvasana Basti or medicated oil should be retained in the body for the duration of three Yama that is nine hours (one Yama= three hours). If Pratyagamana (return of Basti) occurs before this, then another Anuvasana Basti should be administered. If it does not occur even after this period, then one should wait for Ahoratra that is twenty-four hours. In case of no Pratyagamana even after this time, Phalavarti or Tikshna Basti should be administered. Vagbhat Acharya have mentioned that if the Pratyagamana does not occur due to excessive dryness of Koshtha and if there are no any Jadyadi Vikaras then this should be neglected.

Pathya and administration of other Basti:

After Basti Pratyagamana, intake of food should be avoided at that night. On the next day, food should be given during the day and in the evening if the patient has good appetite. Patient should be administered with Koshna Jala or Dhanyaka and Sunthi Siddha Jala on the next day morning. This helps to stimulate the digestive power and produces desire for food. Thereafter, on second, third or fifth day, Anuvasana Basti should be given. After that, Niruha Basti and Anuvasana Basti should be provided on the third and fifth day of every week. According to Acharya Vagbhata, if the patient has a decent appetite after Basti Pratyagamana, a light meal might be given in the evening.

Matra basti

Matra Basti is always useful for persons emaciated by Karma, Vyayama, Bhara, Adhva, Vyavaya and for persons who are Durbala and afflicted with Vataja Vikaras. It can be safely administered in all Ritu without any restrictions of food and specificity of work. It is a form of Anuvasana Basti which promotes the strength and helps in easy elimination of stool. It causes nourishment and cures different Vataja Vikaras

- ....*Seelaneeya sada cha sa:*

  Bala vrudha adhwa bhara stree vyayamaasakti chintakai:
  Vata bhagna abala alpagni nrupeswara sukhatmabhi:
  Doshaghno nishpareeharo balya: srushtamala: sukha: (Ah Su 19/ 67)
  Dose

- *Hraswaya snehapanasya matraya yojita sama:*

  Matravasti : smruta: sneha (Ah Su 19/67)

- *yamadwaya jaranalakshanaya snehapanamatraya sama:* (Sa Su)
- But Su- 1 ½ pala (......kaneeyasya ardhapala...)
- In matra vasti, 1 pala is the minimum dose, 1 ½ pala is the medium and 2 pala is the maximum dose (Ka. Sam)

CHAPTER IX

Uttarabasti

- Uttaravasti is a method to introduce medicine into the genito- urinary tract.
- It is administered during artavakala (ovulation period) in females.
- *Sneho anuvasanavat sodhano niruhavat* – it has properties of both anuvasana and niruha basti
- Vidhi and parihara etc are same as that of anuvasana
- Indicated for diseases related with vasti and garbhasaya.

Definition

- *"Uttaramarga deeyamanataya, kim va sreshtagunataya uttaravasti:"* (Ca Si 9/50- Cakra.)

That which is administered through utaramarga is known as uttaravasti. Utharamarga means mutramarga and sukramarga, ie.penis in male & mutramarga and yonimarga ie.urethral meatus and vaginal orifice in female. The vasti which has very good properties (uttama guna) is uttaravasti.

- *"Gudat uttarena margena medradina deeyata ityuttaravasti:"* (Ah Su 19/1-Sa su)
- *"Niruhat uttaram uttarena va margena deeyata ityuttaravasti:"* (As Su 28/11)
- *"Yastu vasti: mutramargena deeyate sneha: sa uttaravasti:"* (As Su 28/10- Indu)

Classification

- I. On the basis of drugs used- 2 types

Kashayavasti & snehavasti

- II. Acc. To the marga-

yonimarga (garbhasaya vasti) & mutramarga (Mutrasaya vasti)

- III. Usually in females, uthara basti done by three ways

Vaginal douche by kashaya, Vaginal Uttara basti using sneha &Uterine (Intrauterine) Uttara basti using sneha
Uttaravasti putaka

- Aja vasti (Ca)
- *Ourabhra : soukaro va api vasti: aajascha pujita:*

Tadalabhe prayunjeeta galacharma tu pakshinam
(tasyaalabhe drute pado mruducharma tatopi va (Su Ci 37/107)
Ourabhra, mesha, soukara, vanya sookara, aaja;, chagasya vasti: . If they are not available, galacharma of birds or mruducharma of pada is indicated in text. But nowadays animal bladders are not used.
<u>**Uttaravasti netra (Named as pushpanetra)**</u>
For male :
Vagbhata
"Athurangula manena tat netram dwadasangulam
Vruttam gopuchavat mulamadhyayo: krutakarnikam
Sidhardhakapravesagram slakshnm hemadisambhavam

Kunda aswamara sumana: pushpavruntopamam drudam" (Ah Su 19/71-72)

12A (for patients own hand) length , circular, in the shape of gopucha, having 2 karnika- one at the mulabhaga and the other at madhyabhaga (6A from the tip- since size of penis is also about 6 A).

Its lumen should have the size , such a way that a sidhardhaka seed can pass through its tip(size of a mustard seed). Netragra having the shape of kundaaswamara sumana vrunta; and must be drudam

Caraka

Made of gold/ silver; slakshnam

- *Jaaathi aswahanavruntena samam gopuchasamsthitam*
- *Hareeta-kundasya vruntapratimam tatha agre*

12 A, lumen- sarshapachidram

2 karnika- Vastibandhanartham ekata: karnika, apara agre sepha: pramana shadanguladou karnika kartavya:

- 3 karnika- patabhedam
- It should be made of gold , silver, and should be smooth. Should be similar to gopucha in shape, and its tip should have the size of flower stalk of jati and aswahana.
- (Pushpayor vruntena agre samam, Aswahana-karaveera.)
- "Vastibandhanartham ekata: karnika, apara agre sepha: pramana shadanguladou karnika kartavya:" - one at the base for tying vasti putaka and the other should be at the distance of size of sepha from the tip. To limit the insertion thru mutramarga

Susruta

- *Chaturdasangulam netram athurangulasammitam*

  malatee pushpa vruntagram chidram sarshapanirgamam (Su Ci 37/101)
  14 A

- *Nivishtakarnikam madhye* (37/103)
- *Jateepushpavrintasadrusaagram* *sarshapachidram* *madhyasannivishtakarnikam* *suvarnaadimayam* *mule* *dwikarnikam cha* (Dal.37/101)- 3 karnika
- Tantraantare- ...sidharthakapravesagram, mule madhye sakarnikam ....

For Female

- 10 A

- *"Pushpanetrapramanam tu pramadanam dasangulam*

  Mutrasrota: parinaham mudgasroto anuvahi cha" (Ca Si 9/65)

- *"Netram dasangulam mudgapravesam"* (Ah Su 19/79,AS)

  Vruttam, gopuchakaram, mutrasrota parinaham

- **2 karnika**

- *Chaturangulat cha urdhwam karnika karyaa, adhikapravesa nivaaranaartham* (Sa Su)- 4 A from tip-
- *Pravesaavadhou karnika karya ityartha sidham* (Ah Su- AR)

10 A lenghth, in the size/ circumference of mutrasrota: (pushpavruthopamam tu atra na yujyate- sa su.), lumen of its tip should be in a size – through which a mudga seed / green gram can pass through.

One is situated 4 A from tip- to prevent over insertion of netra

- *Nareenam chaturangule iti nivishtakarnikam ityatra* ...(Su ci 37/103 dal.)
- *Mutrasrota: parinaham mudgavahi dasangualm ,Medrayama samam kechid ichanti khalu tadvida:* (Su ci 37/103)
- *Apatyamarge purushendriya sthulam netram kechid adhikachidram cha* (Dal.)
- Trikarnikena netrena ....(su ci 37/115)- for vastinibandhanam, karnikadwayam

Susruta also has the same opinion. But susruta says that according to some other acharyas, netra which is inserting through apatyamarga should have the size of Penis.

3 karnika are mentioned, 2 for vastibandhana and other to limit the insertion

Insertion of netra

<u>For male</u>

- 6A – to be inserted
- Karnika at madhyabhaga of 12A netra; medra- 6A length (Ah)
- *Aamehanantham* (AS)
- *Sephapramana shadanguladou karnika* (Ca Si 9/-Cakra.)
- ....*Vidadhyat angulani shat*...(6A) *medrayamasamam kechidichanti pranidhanakam*(Su ci 37/111)

- *saptangulam cha paramam pranidhanam-* (Su ci 37/ 101-tantraantare)
- Ksharapani- *angulyanyatha chatwari, pancha shat sapta va tatha. Saptangulam param netram pranidheyam bhishakvidaa. Himsyat vastim naram cheha pramaanaat adhikam tata:* (Su ci 37/101)
- Maximum is 7 A, beyond that it will destroy vasti .
- The male urethra is about 17-23 cm length. So by 7A, giving medicine in mid urethral region can produce rupture and leakage. By using foleys catheter , we can do intra bladder uttaravasti

For Female

- *Apatyamarge nareenam vidheyam chaturangulam*

Dwyangulam mutramarge tu balayastu ekamangulam (Ca Si 9/66)

- *Balanam tu apatyamarge na deeyata eva, tamsam apatyamargasya avrutatwat*(Cakrapani)
- *........chaturangulam*

Apatyamarge yojyam syat dwyangulam mutravartmani Mutrakruchravikareshu, balanam tu ekamangulam (Ah Su 19/79,AS)

- *Ya stree surata vyavahara garbhagrahana ayogya , athava ya bala-aprouda, tasyaa yoni:- kevalam mutrasya eva marga: , tasya netram dwyangulam praveshyam. Ata urdhwam tu pravesaat tassam mamsakshati: syat.* (Sa Su)

- In youvanaanaam nareenam- apatyamarge for snehanam- 4 A, mutramarge- sneha-2 A; for bala, *swalpa pramanataya 1A* in mutramarga.
- Yonivibhramsadishu- apatyamarge 4A , and mutrakruchreshu- mutramarge-2A; and for baala- mutramarge-1A
- But by inserting only 1 or 2 A in urethra (of girls and adult women), the end point of nozzle will not be able to cross the internal urethral meatus as urethra is 2-4 cm long. Thus the injection of medicine inside the urinary bladder would be difficult. By inserting only 4A of nozzle inside vaginal canal, the medicine cannot be injected into uterus. If from the word apatyamarga, cervix is considered, instead of vaginal canal, then by inserting 4A inside cervix, the medicine can be injected in the uterus
- *Tasaam apatyamarge tu nidadhyat chaturangulam*

Dwyangulam mutramarge tu kanyanam tu ekamangulam (Su ci 37/104)

- *Streenam artavakale tu yoni: gruhnaati apavrute:*

vidadheeta tada tasmat anrutou api cha atyaye ....(Ah Su 19/77)
Should be administered during artavakala.

- *Rtukala eva artavakala; rtusthu dwadasa nisa; apavaranaat karanaat sneham gruhnaati. Anyada tu samvrutatwat na snehamadatte garbhavat.*

- In women uttaravasti should be administered during artavakala ie. Rtu kala;after menstrual phase; because uterus readily receives or absorbs sneha during this period.But in atyayikavyadhi, like yonivibhramsa sulam, yonivyapt, asrugdaram) any time can be given

Procedure

- **Method of administration in males**

ऋजोः सुखोपवष्टिटस्य पीठे जानुसमे मद्दौ ।
हृष्टे मेढ्रे स्थति चर्जौ शनैः स्रोतोवशिद्धये ॥
सूक्ष्मां शलाकां प्रणयेत्तया शुद्धे अनुसेवनीम्।
आमेहनान्त नेत्रं च नष्किमप गदुवत्ततः ॥
पीडतिऽन्तर्गते स्नेहे स्नेहवस्तकिरमो हतिः ll (AH su.19/75)

- Patient is advised to sit straight on a stool (soft seated) having height equal to knee of patient
- Penis is made to erect and hold straight
- A thin salaka should be inserted slowly to clear the srotas
- If the srotas is found clear, insert the vasti netra carefully along the line of seevani into mutramarga till it transverse full length of penis (aamehanantam)
- Press the putaka uniformly as in gudavasti
- All the regimens of snehavasti has to be followed
- According to A.S. Properties of salaka is mentioned

- मालतीपुष्पवनूताग्र परणिहा घनामृजू श्लक्ष्ण शलाकया.... (AS su.28/56)

- According to Charaka

- ....हृष्टे मेढ्रे घृताक्तया|
शलाकयाऽन्वष्यि गर्ति यद्यप्रतिहिता व्रजेत् l (Ch.Si. 9/56)

- Salaka smeared with ghrita should be inserted to know the route

- शलाकया प्रथममन्वेषणं मार्गवज्ज्ञानार्थम् (Cha.)

Acc to Susruta
स्वभ्यक्तबस्तमिरूधानं तैलेनोष्णेन मानवम् |
पूर्वं शलाकयाऽन्वष्यि ततो नेत्रमनन्तरम् |
शनैः शनैर्घृताभ्यक्तं वदिध्यालानि षट् ||
मेढ्रयामसमं कंचेदिच्छन्ति प्रणधिानकम् |
ततोऽवपीडयेद्बस्ति शनैरैनेत्रं च निर्हरेत् || (Su. Chi.37/111)

- Abhyanga should be done with warm oil on vasti moordha (uparitana bhaga) before the administration of uttaravasti
- And the vasti netra should be smeared with ghee
- It should be slowly introduced for a length of 6 angula or upto whole length of penis
- remove netra slowly

Method of administration in female

- Position of the patient

- उत्तानायाः शयानायाः सम्यक् संकोच्य सक्थिनी।

ऊर्ध्व जान्वा...(Ah su 19/81)

- The women should lie down on her back with flexed knee (lithotomy position) during the procedure

- उत्तानायाः शयानायाः सम्यक् सङ्कोच्य सक्थिनी||६७||

अथास्याः प्रणयेन्नेत्रमनुवंशगतं सुखम्| (Ch si 9/67)

- Vastinetra should be inserted along the direction of vertebral column

ऊर्ध्वजान्वं स्त्रयिं दद्यादुत्तानायं वचिक्षणः |
सम्यक् प्ररपीडयेद्योनिं दद्यात् सुमृदुपीडितिम् |
त्रकिर्णकिने नेत्रेण दद्याद्योनमिखं प्ररति |(Su chi 37/124)

- Vastiputaka should be compressed uniformly

Paschat karma

ततः प्रत्यागतस्नेहमपराह्णे वचिक्षणः |
भोजयेत् पयसा मात्रां यूषेणाथ रसेन वा ||
अनेन वधिनिा दद्याद्बस्तींस्त्रींश्चतुरोऽपि वा | (Su.chi.37/113)

- After the medicine has returned three or four enema should be given
- In the evening after considering the doshas bhojana with ksheera,yusha or mamsarasa should be given

वस्तीननेन वधिनिा दद्यात् त्रींश्चतुरोऽपि वा ||
अनुवासनवच्छेषं सर्वमेवास्य चन्तियेत् । (AH su.19/76)

- paschat karma of snehavasti should be followed

..........त्रचित्रान् अहोरात्रेण योजयेत्
वस्तीस्त्ररिरात्रम् एव ंच स्नेहमात्रा ंविविर्धयन् ।
त्र्यहम् एव च वश्रिम्य प्रणदिध्यात् पुनस्त्र्यहम् ॥ (AH su. 19/82)

- Iike this 3 or 4 uttaravasti should be done in one ahoratra
- It should be continued for 3 days in which the dose of Sneha Should be increased gradually
- After taking rest for 3 days it may be administered again for another 3 days

Uttara vasti in current Practice

- Mutrashayagata Uttara vasti/ intra vescical UV

Requirements:

- Table for administration
- Cleaning agents like Savlon, Betadine etc.
- Sponge holding forceps and artery forceps ,Sterile gauze, Surgical towel & towel clips
- Sterile gloves, kidney tray,steel bowl
- Anesthetic gel (Xylocaine 2%)
- Urinary rubber / disposable catheter No. 6-8

- Aspiration syringe(disposable)
- Medicated oil, decoction selected according to the condition
- Autoclave facility

- Garbhashayagata uttaravasti

The following may be taken as uttaravasti netra for **intra uterine** administration.
1. I.V cannula
2. Ruben's canula/ Intrauterine insemination cannula
3. Urinary rubber catheter no. 11 or 12

- A 10 ml syringe may be used as vastiputaka
- Cusco's bivalve speculum- for proper visualization of cervix
- Uterine sound – to know the position of uterus
- Cleaning agents like Savlon, Betadine etc.
- Sponge holding forceps and artery forceps ,Sterile gauze, Surgical towel & towel clips, sterile cotton
- Sterile gloves, kidney tray
- Medicated sneha- autoclaved

Intravaginal UV

- Cusco's bivalve speculum
- Disposable Syringe -25 ml capacity

Intravesical UV in male
Pre-operative Procedure

- All the instruments used during the procedure including the medicine have to be autoclaved and kept ready.
- Patient is examined for the parameters like BP, pulse, temperature etc. before he is put to table.
- Remove pubic hair before the procedure
- Do abhyanga and ushma sweda over pelvic and lumbo sacral regions
- Patient must lie down on supine position on the clean table by exposing the part.

- Wash the genitalia and the surrounding area with antiseptic solution by using sponge holding forceps & gauze.
- The physician should wear the gloves after washing hands
- Retract the prepuce completely and wash thoroughly the glans penis & then apply Betadine to glans penis
- spread the surgical towel over patient, exposing the penis. Towel clips may be applied.
- When once the assistant transfers the autoclaved medicine into steel bowl the medicine is filled in to the syringe.
- Smear distal portion of the catheter with sneha / xylocaine gel

Operative Procedure

- Gently introduce the catheter in to the urethra; slowly introduce the catheter into the bladder until urine starts to flow
- Drain urine completely
- Inflate balloon, using correct amount of sterile liquid
- Gently pull catheter until inflated balloon is snug against bladder neck
- Then slowly inject the medicine taken in 30 ml syringe into the catheter.
- If more amount of medicine has to be injected clamp the catheter with artery forceps, remove the syringe & then inject the medicine with the same syringe or by another

Post Operative procedure

- When once the injection of medicine is over deflate balloon by draining sterile water
- then remove the catheter & allow the patient to lie down in the same position for 5 to 10 minutes.
- Check the tip of the catheter to ensure that there is no bleeding
- Clean the glans and meatus again

Intravesical UV in females

- Similar procedure
- Patient should lie in lithotomy position
- Spread labia and lift up
- Clean urethral opening using downward strokes

Intra vaginal & intra uterine UV
Pre-Operative procedure

- Yoniprakshalana should be done with suitable antiseptic lotion/kashaya.
- All the instruments used during the procedure including the medicine have to be autoclaved and kept ready.
- Remove pubic hair before the procedure
- Ask the patient to void urine
- The patient is examined for the parameters like BP, pulse, temperature etc before she is put to table
- Do abhyanga and ushma sweda over pelvic and lumbo sacral regions

Operative procedure

- Then the patient is kept in lithotomy position with the part exposed, cleaned and draped.

- The part is covered with the ring towel and only the perineum is exposed.
- Later the lubricated cuscus speculum is slowly inserted to expose the cervix.
- Cervix and the surrounding areas are cleaned with suitable antiseptic lotions.

For intra vaginal UV

- Medicine should be pushed carefully into vagina using a 25 ml syringe
- Remove speculum after injection of medicine

For intra uterine UV

- The direction of the uterus can be understood by the insertion of uterine sound.
- In case of closed internal os, Hegars dialator may be used.
- The autoclaved sneha is then taken in the 10 ml syringe, then attach it to intra uterine insemination canula.
- The canula is carefully introduced to the uterus through the cervix (after removing the air bubble) and the medicine is pushed in slowly taking 2- 3 minutes

Post operative procedure

- The patient has to lie down for 30 minutes in head low position- for retaining medicine

Retention of uttaravasti dravya

- Acc to Gayadasa (Bhaluki darsanam) the pratyagamana kala of snaihika uttaravasti dravya is 100 matra kala
- बसूतरि्मात्राशतादरूध्वं पूरत्यागच्छति
- Acc to Dridhabala pratyagamana kala of uttara vasti is similar to that of anuvasana ie.3 yama
- In practice kashāyas are used as vaginal douche alone and not for intra uterine administration
- It is observed that kvatha returns out immediately where as sneha is retained for sometime
- Retention time ranges between three to six hours or upto next reflex of voiding – in intra vesical UV
- **Precautions and aseptic measures**
- Try to use disposable instruments
- All instruments including sneha (oil/ ghee) medicine should be autoclaved to avoid infections
- Freshly prepared kashaya (decoction) & ksheerapaka (medicated milk) can be used directly
- The medicine is checked for luke warm temperature before administration
- The catheter/canula should not be forcefully inserted in case any obstruction is met
- Instillation of medicaments should be slow and gentle
- Rectum and bladder should be empty.
- External genitalia is ensured as clean
- For intra uterine UV, Patient should be kept in O.T. under strict aseptic conditions
- Care should be taken to prevent fat embolism and peritonitis- only 3 to 5 ml should be injected
- If quantity is more than 10 ml it may cross fallopian tube and enter peritoneum causing peritonitis
- While cleaning urethral orifice in female, downward strokes (front to back) should be used with a cotton ball

soaked in antiseptic solution

Complications & it's management

1. Pranidhana dosha

- हस्यिादतगितंबस्तमिनूसे्नहोनगच्छ्तर्ा|
सुख्ं प्ररपीड्य नष्किम्प ंनष्किर्षेन्ननेत्रमेव च (Ch.Si. 9/56)
- If the vasti netra inserted beyond the prescribed limit it will cause injury to the bladder
- If it is inserted lesser than the limit the sneha will not enter the bladder
- So insert the vasti netra carefully without trembling the hands and press the putaka gently

2. Apratyagamana of vastidravya

- If vasti dravya isn't returned within 100 matra,in the absence of any complications it can be neglected.
- अनागच्छन्ननरिुपद्रवश्चाहोरात्रमुपेक्षणीय (Dalhana)
- If it is upadravakari, it has to be explled out with varti prayoga, teekshna sodhana vasti etc (Su.Chi.37/117)
- Kashaya of Sodhana gana dravya (trivridadi/ trinapanchamuladi gana dravya)should be used as Niruhauttara vasti in the dose of 1 and 2 Prasruta in Mutra and Yoni Marga respectively
- Sodhana gana dravya siddha guda varti should be inserted
- Salaka should be inserted in mutramarga
- Abdomen is to be pressed forcefully below the umbilicus with clenched fist
- Aragwadhadi varti prayoga (Su chi 37/120)

- Prepared by triturating Aragwadha Patra with Nirgundi swarasa, Gomutra and Saindhava and dried in shade, smeared with Ghee and inserted into Mutamarga with the help of Salaka
- Varti should be prepared in a size of Mudga, Ela or Sarshapa according to age
- In yoni marga- large varti in a size of 4 angula
- Agaradhumadi varti (su chi 37/122)
- Prepared with agaradhuma, brhati, pippali,madana phala, saindhava and nagara, triturated either in sukta, gomutra or sura may be introduced through urethra

3. Daha

शर्करामधुमश्रिरेण शीतेन मधुकाम्बुना
दह्यमाने तदा बस्तौ दद्याद्बस्तर्ि वचिक्षण: |
क्षीरवृक्षकषायेण पयसा शीतलेन च l (Su.chi.37/123)

- Burning sensation produced by vitiated pitta, after administering teekshna & ushna vasti (for elimination of apratyagata sneha) (Dalhana)
- Vasti with sarkara & madhu mixed in seeta kashaya of Yashti madhu
- Ksheeravriksha seeta kashaya + Ksheera for vasti

In practise, complications found can be categorized as

- Immediate complications : Shock ,Pain, contusion, urethral/vaginal rupture, cervical laceration , endometrial trauma, fat embolism
- Late complications : Peritonitis,Infection , cystitis, UTI, fever, endometriosis

1.Shock (Neurological): Neurological shock may be due to the forceful insertion of Rubber Catheter in Urethra and in spinchter of Urinary bladder or forceful insertion of speculum in vagina or a patient in anxious mood.

- This condition needs immediate resuscitation or else may be life threatening.

2.Pain (Spasmodic): Pain may be due to the forceful insertion in Urethra or vagina

- It is usually self limiting and if necessary antispasmodics can be given

3. Rupture /contusion/ Cervical laceration /Endometrial trauma - occurs while insertion

- Vranahara treatment

4. Peritonitis: If the medicine is forcefully pushed it may spill in to peritoneal cavity through fallopian tube, leading to cause inflammation

- Needs anti-inflammatory medicines

5. Infection: The source of infection may be either through the improper sterilization of the instrument or medicament or poor aseptic precautions during the procedure.

- Require a course of antibiotic therapy and a good nursing care

6. Cystitis/UTI/fever- due to poor aseptic precautions during the procedure.

- Symptomatic treatment can be given

7. Uterine distention -If procedure is done with high pressure or dose of medicine is more

- Due to uterine distention severe pain in lower abdomen, backache, shoulder pain will be occurred

Dose

For male

- Sneha- ½ pala (for 25 years of age)
- *Yatha vayo viseshena snehamatram vikalpya va* (Ca Si 9/52)
- *Tasya vasti: mrudulaghu: matra sukti: vikalpya va* (Ah Su 19/72, AS)

Sukti- (karshadwayam- ½ pala)- for sneha

- *Vayorbala deha satwa satmyadi vasaat nirupya va matra* (Sa Su)
- *Doshadi apekshaya nyunam adhikam va* (AR)
- 3 or 4 uttaravasti should be performed
- ½ pala is the dose for 25 yrs of age. Caraka does not give the dose for male and female separately. Dose depends on age.
- Ah, AS-*vastirdravya adharo mrudurlaghuscha. Doshadeen vikalpya matra.*
- For snaihika- *paramam prakuncha:*

- For below 25 years- *vidadhyat budhikalpitam* (Su Ci37/ 102)
- Kharanada- ½ pala- 2, 3 uttaravastis.

For female

- *Prakuncho madhyama matraa, baalaanam suktireva tu* (Ah Su 19/80,AS)

- (for sneha- madhyama matra- 1 pala for stree, and ½ pala for baala)

- *Dwistri chaturiti snehan ahoratrena yojayet...*

  ....triratram karma kurveeta snehamatram vivardhayet
  Anena eva vidhanena karma kuryat puna: tryahaat (Ca Si 9/68)

- twice/thrice or 4 times in a day ,(3, 4 times in a day- AH) for 3 days. Then rest for next 3 days,and again in the same manner uttaravasti should be done for next three days. Pratyaham snehamatra vardhayet

- *Snehasya prasrutam cha atra swaangulimoola sammitam*

  Deyam pramanam paramam arvag budhivikalpitham (Su Ci 37/106)

- Dal- *swaangulimulasammita: prasruto deya:- taccha uttamam pramanam sarva vayo avsthasuu baleeyasi roge, madhyaheena bala roge tu sarvasu api vayo avasthasu uthamapramanaat arvak madhyam heenam cha budhya vikalpitham.....*

- *Niruhottaravasti pramana-Su Ci 37/116)*
- *Kwathapramanam prasrutam, striya dwiprasrutam bhavet*
- *Kanyetarasyaa:, kanyaya: tadwat vastipramanakam*
- For male- *swahasta sammita prasrutam*
- Female- *garbhagrahanayogyaya-garbhasayasodhanartham, vasti sodhanartham- dwiprasruta* (swahasta)
- Kanya- *aprapta dwadasavarsha- swahastasammita prasrutam-* for vasti sodhanam
- Uttara Basti using kashaya – the dose is mentioned only by Sushruta. Vagbhata has not specificallynmentioned any kashaya for Uttara Basti. Caraka also has not clearly described the dosage it is mentioned that dose of kashaya should be decided upon the condition. (for adult also- for urinary bladder, 1 prasruta)

Acharya	• Male	• Stree	• Baala
Vagbhata	½ pala	1 pala	½ pala
Charaka	½ pala	½ pala	------
Susrutha	1 pala- max- sneha 1 Prasruta – kwatha	1 prasruta – sneha 2 prasruta – kwatha	1 prasruta- kwatha
Sa. Sam& BP	----------	Sneha-2 pala- apatyamarga, 1 pala mutramarga	2 karsha (1/2 pala)

Uttarabasti-dose

Practical dose

<u>For Sneha</u>

- Vaginal - 100ml (30 ml)
- Urinary- 50ml , young girls- 25ml
- Intravaginal - 3-5ml/ 5-10ml (maximum 10ml)
- If >10ml is given, it may cross the fallopian tube and may enter into the peritoneum causing peritonitis.

<u>For kashaya</u>

- Vaginal-200ml
- Urinary- 100ml
- (Douche- 2 L)

Indication

- *Doshadhikyamavekshya ethan mutrakruchraharai: jayet*

  vastim uttaravastim cha sarveshameva daapayet (Ca Si 9/ 49)

- In all 13 types of mutraroga Indication

- *Doshadhikyamavekshya ethan mutrakruchraharai: jayet*

  vastim uttaravastim cha sarveshameva

- *Vastijeshu vikareshu yonivibhramsajeshu cha*

  Yonisuleshu teevreshu yonivyapatsu asrugdare
  Aprasravati mutre cha bindum bindum sravatyapi
  Vidadhyat uttaram vasti: yadhasu oushadhasamskrutam (Ca Si 9/63-64)

- *Vastou rogeshu nareenam yonigarbhasayeshu cha*

Dwitrasthapana sudhebhyo vidadhyat vastimuttaram(Ah Su 19/70, As Su28/55)

- *Yonivibhramsa suleshu yonivyapat asrugdare* (Ah Su 19/78,AS)

- *Snigdham vantam viriktam cha nirudamanuvasitam*

  Yojayet sukradoshaartam samyak uttaravastina (Su Sa 2/11)

- *Sukram dushtam sonitam cha anganaanaam*

  Pushpodrekam tasya nasam cha kashtam
  Mutraghataat mutradoshan pravrudhan
  Yonivyadhim samsthiti cha aparaya:
  Sukrotsekam sarkaram asmarim cha
  Sulam vastou vamkshane mehane cha
  Ghoran anyan vastijamscha api rogan
  Hitwa mehan uttaro hanti vasti: (Su Ci 37/125)

In Sushruta chikitsa,he points out that Uttara basti can be administered in severe conditions affecting vasti and yoni. It is also useful in sukradosha, artavadosha, mutraghata, asmari, and pain in regions of bladder, groin and penis.

Contraindications

In males
Uretral stricture
Bleeding disorder
Carcinoma of bladder
Carcinoma of penis
Hypo/ epispadiasis
In females

Intrauterine Uttar Basti

Hypersensitivity

Carcinoma of cervix

Heavy bleeding

Virginity

Vesicovaginal fistula

Intravaginal uttar basti

Hypersensitivity

Menorrhagia

Retrovaginal fistula

MODE OF ACTION OF UTTARABASTI

Purvakarma

Snehan and Swedan are significant panchakarma procedures that serve as both pradhan and purva karma. Uttar Basti deals with Apan Vayu, which has its seat in nearby organs. Prior to Uttar Basti, Snehan and Swedan perform anuloman, resulting in increased efficacy. Additionally, performing vatanuloman before the treatment reduces the risk of problems. Snehan and Swedana prior to Uttar Basti help relax stomach muscles. Relaxation is crucial for Uttar Basti to prevent uterine irritation and reduce pain during and after the surgery. Yoni prakshalana should be taken before Uttar Basti, along with an antibiotic.

Pradhan karma

Mode of action of Uttar Basti can be understood in two ways.

Local effect of Uttar Basti :

The effectiveness of Uttar Basti varies depending on the method, equipment, and medicine employed. If administered through the cervical canal, the medication may have a greater impact on cervical variables. For cervical stenosis, a katu ushana taila-based medication can be beneficial. For boosting mucus output from cervical glands, a nutritional and Madhur-shita ghrita-based medicine is more effective. Similarly, medication selection for ovulatory and tubal factors varied significantly. The drug's action on the ovary occurs after it is absorbed and promotes the presence of hypothalamic arteries. On ovary the effect of drug will be after absorption and then by promoting the Hypothalamic – Pitutary–Ovarian axis. While in the tubal block, Uttar Basti operates locally. A medicine with snehan properties can be beneficial during ovulation, but a drug with Lekhana karma is preferable for tubal blockage. Uttar Basti may also trigger certain endometrial receptors, resulting in the correction of all reproductive physiological processes. Intravaginal Uttar Basti may also facilitate medication absorption since the posterior fornix has a highly abundant blood supply and may act as a store of drug.

Systemic effects

Ayurveda distinguished between oral and parenteral medicine administration since its inception. Uttar Basti may stimulate some nuroendocrine pathways after absorption.The impact of Uttar Basti on the system can be studied using systemic biology concepts. Systemic biology is a new and widely acknowledged concept in current science. This philosophy takes a comprehensive approach, recognizing the molecular connections between all biological systems and organs. Any changes in one organ's molecular level will affect the others. This thought was the initial step towards modern science's understanding of Mahabhut and Tridosha. The effect of Uttar Basti drugs have on the physiology of reproductive system, it will definitely involve the physiological functions and corrections of other organs.

Abbreviations

Ah/A.Hr : Ashtanga Hridayam
Ca/Cha : Caraka samhita
Su : Susruta Samhita
Sa : Sharngadhara samhita
Cakra : cakrapani
Dal : Dalhana
Ka : Kashyapa Samhita
Su : Sutra sthana
Chi : Chikitsa sthana
Kal : Kalpa sthana
Si : Sidhi sthana
Acc : According to

Bibliography

1. Ghanekar BG, Vaidya L. Sushrut Samhita. Motilal Banarsidass Publishe; 2007.
2. Samhita C. Charaka Samhita. Vols I--VI, Jamnagar, India: Shree Gulab Kunverba Ayurvedic Society. 1949.
3. Garde G., Sartha Vagbhata, reprint 2012 edition, Varanasi: Choukhamba SurbharatiPrakashana; 2017
4. Ashtanghrudayam, commentaries of Sarvangsundara of Arunadatta and Ayurved rasayana of Hemadri, edited by Pandit Hari Sadashiv Shastri Paradkara ;chaukhamba prakashan ,2010,
5. Acharya Harita of Harita Samhita, by Ramavallabha Shastri, first edition, Shastha Sharira Sthana, Varanasi, Prachya Prakashana, 1985,
6. Kashyap Samhita, edited by Shri Satyapal Bhishagacharya with hindi commentary Vidyotini, Reprint edition, Choukhmbha Sanskrit Series, Varanasi
7. Sharangadhara, Sharangadhara Samhita,Choukhambha Surbharti Prakashan, Varanasi, Reprint 2013,
8. M.R.Vasudevan Nampoothiri and L.Mahadevan, Principles and practice of basti, 3rd edition,
9. Savrikar SS, Lagad CE. Study of Preparation and Standardization of 'Maadhutailika Basti' with special reference to Emulsion Stability. Ayu. 2010 Jan;31(1):1-6. doi: 10.4103/0974-8520.68190. PMID: 22131675; PMCID: PMC3215309.
10. Gurjar RS, Gokhale mv. mode of action of panchtikta ksheera basti in dhatukshayajanya sandhigata vata: conceptual study.
11. Yogita B, Lekurwale P, Mekhale S, Rathode S, K D GC. A

"

critical review on pharmacodynamics of Basti Chikitsa and its action on enteric nervous system. Int J Ayurvedic Med. 2015 Sep 1;6(4).

12. Vd. Sarvesh Kumar Singh & Vd. Kshipra Rajoria, A Textbook of Panchakarma, Varanasi, Chaukhamba Prakashan, chapter no, 520.

13. Anup Jain. A textbook of panchakarma, New Delhi : Jaypee brothers medical publishers : Reprint, 2019. chapter, 40

Author Details

Vd Vrushali santosh Swami

Accomplished professional with a Bachelor's degree from Amravati University, graduating in 1999, and a Master's degree in Kayachikitsa from Shivaji University, Kolhapur, completed in 2004. Brings over 20 years of experience in teaching and clinical practice. Specializing in Panchakarma, Kayachikitsa, and counselling psychology, has also completed a postgraduate degree in counselling psychology. Throughout this career, guided numerous postgraduate students, helping to shape the next generation of Ayurvedic professionals. Additionally, books and numerous research articles have been published, along with presentations at various national and international seminars. Currently serving as the Head of the Department and Professor in Panchakarma department at MES Ayurveda Mahavidyalaya in Ratnagiri, Maharashtra.

Vd Santosh Irayya Swami

Completed graduation in 1998 with distinction and earned a postgraduate degree in Kayachikitsa in 2004 from Shivaji University, Kolhapur. Currently serves as an Associate Professor at S.G.R Ayurveda College in Solapur, recognized as a well-known physician with 20 years of teaching and clinical experience. Has authored several books and published numerous research articles, along with presented papers at various national and international seminars. Currently pursuing a PhD and involved in ongoing AYUSH-funded research projects, further contributing to the field of Ayurveda.

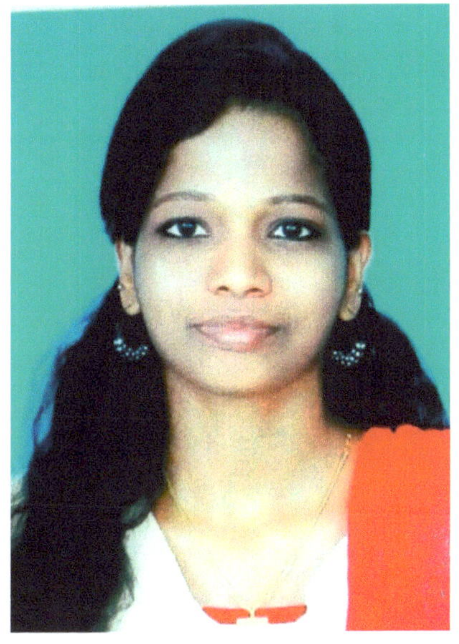

Vd Aswathi C K

Completed a Bachelor of Ayurvedic Medicine and Surgery (BAMS) from Government Ayurveda College, Kannur, Kerala in 2018 and a postgraduate degree in Panchakarma from VPSV Ayurveda College, Kottakkal, Kerala in 2022. With 2 years of teaching and clinical experience, specializing in Keraliya Panchakarma procedures, has published articles and presented papers at national and international seminars. Currently works as an Assistant Professor in the Department of Panchakarma at MES Ayurveda Mahavidyalaya, Ratnagiri (MH).

www.ingramcontent.com/pod-product-compliance
Lightning Source LLC
Chambersburg PA
CBHW040908110726
48005CB00006B/830